# True Stories

## of Baseball's Hall of Famers

David Kellogg

A Bluewood Book

This edition produced and published by Bluewood Books
A Division of The Siyeh Group, Inc.
P.O. Box 689
San Mateo, CA  94401

ISBN 0-912517-41-7

Printed in U.S.A.
10, 9, 8, 7, 6, 5, 4, 3, 2, 1

Editor: Tony Napoli
Designer: Kevin Harris

ABOUT THE AUTHOR:
David Kellogg is a sports journalist. He has covered a variety of professional sports teams for American and foreign publications, and is currently a sports editor for a major Bay Area newspaper. He lives in the San Francisco area with his wife and two children.

PHOTO CREDITS:
All photographs in this book are furnished courtesy of The National Baseball Hall of Fame Library, Cooperstown, NY

# Table Of Contents

# Introduction

There is a scene in the movie *Field of Dreams* where a young, fresh-faced kid looks at the ball players who have come back to life on this Iowa ball field and speaks in awestruck tones.

"Hey, that's Smoky Joe Wood, and Mel Ott, and Walter Johnson."

Shoeless Joe Jackson, one of the other player-apparitions, says, "Ty Cobb wanted to play, but none of us could stand him when he was alive, so we told him to stick it."

I laughed at that remark, and then turned to my wife. She was giving me that look—a tilt of the head with a slight squint—that told me she didn't get the joke and wasn't really sure if she wanted to.

I started to explain that Cobb could be a downright dirty player and was just a nasty guy to boot. But by that time I was talking over the movie's next scene, and well, my wife was nodding her head, but also motioning back to the screen: "Don't ruin the movie."

I realized that when the boy named off the players, all members of the Baseball Hall of Fame, they were just names to my wife. (All members of the Hall except of course Shoeless Joe, who along with seven other players, was banned from baseball for taking money from gamblers to throw the 1919 World Series.) However, when I heard the names, they were much more than that. I thought of the people, or rather the many stories I'd heard about them that told me so much more than their career statistics. I knew that Mel Ott was one of the most prolific home run hitters in history, but I also knew that Ott was one of the best loved players and managers of his time. And it had been Ott, of whom the hard-nosed player-manager Leo Durocher referred to when he disdainfully uttered the immortal words, "Nice guys finish last."

So I could imagine Ott being invited to

play, and Cobb being given the cold shoulder.

What I've tried to do within the pages of this book, is to describe the stories that go behind all the statistics, the home runs, the RBIs, the no-hitters, and tell about ballplayers—what made them great, what they had to overcome to achieve greatness, what were their moments of truth. Oh, it's easy to pick up a book and see that Hank Aaron is the all-time leading home run hitter; or that Ted Williams hit .406 in only his third major league season; or that Christy Mathewson once won three games in a World Series, all complete game shutouts. However, it tells us so much more about the men to know what they went through—their fears, their struggles, and their hopes— to reach these athletic heights.

Not every Hall of Famer is included in this book; but you will find a wide cross-section of players, representing every era of the 20th century, from nearly every franchise in major league history.

My hope is that as you read through these pages, the people described within them will come alive, and that should you come across their names again—with all their lifetime statistics of hits, home runs, batting averages, wins, losses, stolen bases—these names will mean just a little more to you than a lot of numbers and letters on a page. **TS**

**Shoeless Joe Jackson**

Connie Mack

# The Tall Tactician

Connie Mack had heard ballplayers like Howard Ehmke pleading for their jobs before. This had been the hardest part of his job as manager and part-owner of the Philadelphia Athletics—he had to tell players when it was time to go. So it pained Mack to hear Ehmke begging for a chance to pitch in the 1929 World Series.

On the surface, Mack was a stern task master, a man who fired a pitcher for "not trying" and scolded another for cursing. On his way to winning nine pennants and five World Championships as the manager of the Athletics, Mack wore a dark suit and tie in the dugout and directed players in the field by waving his scorecard.

However, beneath the surface, Mack was a man of immense patience who did not let his ego stand in the way of doing what was best for his team. Mack was called the Tall Tactician, but the real reason for his longevity in baseball—he played and managed for an unheard of 66 years —was his ability to work with people.

Ehmke stood before him as the 1929 season was drawing to a close, with the Athletics having clinched the pennant and scheduled to play in the World Series. Ehmke was the team's fourth best starting pitcher, a 14-year veteran who seemed on his way out. He had pitched only 55 innings so far, and had not appeared during this last month of the regular season. He arrived in Mack's office and pleaded for a chance to pitch in the Series.

"Do you think you have one game left?" Mack asked.

"I know I do," Ehmke answered.

Mack thought for a minute, then told his veteran pitcher, "All right. Stay here in Philadelphia while we're in the west (on a road trip) and get ready for the Cubs (the eventual National League pennant winner). Scout them when they come to play the Phillies. Work out every day, and be ready for the first game of the Series."

Mack kept his plan secret until the very last moment. When Ehmke went to the mound to start game one, sportswriters, fans, and even teammates were shocked.

Mack's move had appeared to be purely sentimental, but there was more to it than that. The Cubs were a team that ate up fastballs, but had trouble with off-speed pitches—junk balls. Ehmke had a good slow curve that kept hitters off balance. Mack's strategy paid off to perfection. Ehmke struck out a series record 13 batters and recorded a complete game 3-1 victory.

Ehmke would retire early the next season. However, he had justified Mack's faith in him. His "one good game left" had started the A's on their way to winning the 1929 Series—the first of the final two World Championships the A's would win under their brilliant manager. **TS**

## The Judge Who Ruled Baseball

Judge Kenesaw Mountain Landis knew in his heart that the decisions he made were the right ones, no matter what a jury might say, or another judge, or even a darned baseball player.

So as he sat in those August days of 1921, going over and over again the evidence in the Chicago "Black" Sox scandal, he knew his decree on the matter was going to supersede anything a court might rule. In major league baseball, there was no higher court in the land than that of Judge Landis. And Landis, who was named after a civil war battle site where his father had been wounded, just knew that this was the way it was destined to be—just as he had been destined to be a judge.

After all, no one back home could have imagined that Landis—who had dropped out of high school—would one day become the most powerful man in baseball. However, something had driven him to study law, and succeed in it. In 1905, President Theodore Roosevelt, perhaps sensing in the hard-driving, fearless style of Landis a kindred spirit, appointed him a federal judge. And, indeed, Landis backed down from no one—including the rich and powerful John D. Rockefeller, whose Standard Oil company Landis fined $29 million in a court case in 1907.

In 1920, major league baseball owners realized they needed someone with the kind of grit and sense of frontier justice Landis possessed. Although the sport was extremely popular and had tremendous money-making potential, it was being torn apart by gambling and internal squabbling. There were plenty of horses to pull this money cart, but they were all going in different directions. Baseball needed someone to harness and put the whip to them. The owners offered that job to Landis.

In the summer of 1921, eight Chicago White Sox players who allegedly had taken money from gamblers to throw the 1919 World Series, were brought to trial. The nation's baseball fans just wearily shook their heads, as none of the gamblers were charged and none were called to testify. In the middle of the case, the prosecution admitted it had lost confessions and waivers of immunity signed by three players. On Aug. 2, the jury found the players not guilty.

Landis was ready for just such an announcement. The next morning his office banned the players:

"Regardless of the verdict of juries, no player that throws a ball game; no player that undertakes or promises to throw a ball game; no player that sits in a conference with a bunch of crooked players and gamblers where the ways and means of throwing games are planned and discussed and does not promptly tell his club about it, will ever play professional baseball. . . . Baseball is entirely competent to protect itself against crooks, both inside and outside the game."

It was the first of many times that Landis would make tough, controversial decisions. Of course, Landis and everyone else knew that he was baseball, and that his decision would stand no matter who challenged or questioned it. None of the players ever played major league baseball again.

Landis would rule baseball until 1944, when at the age of 78, he died in office. He would take on the biggest stars in baseball, including Babe Ruth, who he once suspended for embarking on an unsanctioned barnstorming tour. For more than 20 years, in baseball Judge Landis would always have the final say. **TS**

# The Day Cy Young Was Perfect

Even in 1904, there was old school and new school. Cy Young was old school. He was a 37-year old right-handed pitcher for the Boston Braves. He was as dependable as the sunrise, a pitcher who didn't care about strikeouts, only getting the batter out using as few pitches as possible.

Young was one of baseball's first truly great pitchers, a man who had already won more than 25 games a season ten times. However, now he was at the crest of his career, about to start the slow slide down.

Rube Waddell was new school, a 28-year old left-hander for the Philadelphia A's who specialized in striking people out—and disappearing for days at a time. Where Cy Young believed in rigorous, scientific conditioning, Waddell seemed to put his faith in fishing trips and barroom rounds.

Yet, in 1904, Young and Waddell had one thing in common. They were the best pitchers in baseball. And when they hooked up for a game on May 5 in Boston, an overflow crowd packed the park.

Young and the Braves were wary of the A's. Just three days before, Waddell had thrown a one-hitter against them. However, beating Young was no picnic either; he would win 26 games that season. Although he wasn't as overpowering as he once was—his fastball having lost a little something—he had compensated for that by developing two other pitches: a curve ball that broke hard toward a right-handed hitter, and another curve that was slower and caught

**Cy Young**

— 13 —

the outside corner of the plate. These pitches didn't blast past batters, so much as make a tempting offer that resulted in ground outs and pop-ups.

In the early innings against the A's, their players flirted with hits, sending weak grounders and fly balls into the gaps. But the Braves' fielders scrambled and kept anything from falling in for a base hit.

Waddell was matching Young scoreless inning after scoreless inning. But in the sixth, the Braves broke through for a run. It was the only run Young would need.

By the seventh inning, the Braves realized they had something special going on. As they took the field, first baseman Candy LaChance told Young, "no one has been by here (first base) yet." Young didn't acknowledge him. Either he didn't hear him, or didn't want to.

By the ninth inning, Boston was leading 3-0. Young retired the first two hitters, then was stunned as Rube Waddell came up to the plate.

Everyone had expected A's manager Connie Mack to pinch-hit for his pitcher. But Mack, with a flair for the dramatic, stuck with Waddell.

It wasn't very dramatic. Waddell took two strikes and then flied out. Young had his perfect game, the first in American League history, and he had done it in just an hour and 23 minutes. The legendary Mack would say it was the greatest pitched game he'd ever seen. Young would go on to win a total of 511 games—the all-time career record—and have baseball's annual award for best pitchers named in his honor. **TS**

# Little Napoleon Finally Gets Respect

John McGraw had whipped and pushed his New York Giants, turning them from an eighth-place team to a pennant winner in just two years. It was 1904 and for McGraw, who had endured more than his share of second-guessing and condemnation, the World Series should have been a showcase for his genius.

But the man they called Little Napoleon had something else in mind. "That's a minor league," McGraw said when reporters asked if he was looking forward to the series against Boston of the American League. "Why should we play them?"

And the Giants didn't. There was no World Series that year, and while baseball fans may have been frustrated, McGraw smiled. It was sweet revenge against Ban Johnson, the founder of the American League, and a man McGraw hated.

This was the same Ban Johnson who had first given McGraw an opportunity to manage. In 1901, McGraw was an aging infielder playing out his career in St. Louis. When Johnson started the American League, he picked McGraw to be the player-manager of the Baltimore Orioles. Only it didn't work out the way either man had hoped.

Oh, McGraw was successful in Baltimore; the fans loved him. However, Johnson wanted McGraw to tow the line. Johnson insisted that McGraw stop second-guessing umpires and causing problems on the field. However, that just wasn't John McGraw's way.

McGraw would become one of the most successful managers of all time, winning 10 pennants in 29 full seasons with the New York Giants, but he did it his way. He bullied, he cajoled, he pushed his players to the limit and some of them beyond. And he didn't seem to care what anyone thought.

Anyone who had seen McGraw play, could foresee how he would manage. McGraw used every trick in the book. He'd slide into a base with his spikes high, at the very least trying to intimidate opponents. Playing third base, he'd subtly grab the belt of a base runner, holding him back when he'd try to tag up and score. However, he was also ingenious and an innovator. He and Wee Willie Keeler first pioneered the strategy of the hit and run.

Like McGraw, Johnson was an egocentric man, focused on becoming a success. At the turn of the century he had taken over a minor-league circuit, added teams and top notch players, changed its name to the American League, and called it a major league. In 1903, the National League recognized the new circuit as a major league and the concept of a season ending series between the leagues—the World Series—was born.

Johnson insisted upon a certain standard of behavior from his players and managers. "Clean ball is the main plank in the American League platform," Johnson preached. "The umpires are agents of the League and must be treated with respect."

However, McGraw was of a different mind. He went after the umpires with a zeal—and paid for it. He was given the thumb by many an umpire. Those umpires, in turn, were given a pat on the back by Johnson.

"I am glad (the umpire ejected) and humiliated McGraw," Johnson said after one such incident. "Rowdyism will not be tolerated ... and the men who disregard the organization rules must suffer the consequences."

Understandably McGraw was furious, so when the lowly New York Giants of the National League came calling, McGraw jumped at the chance to change leagues.

McGraw took over during the 1902 season, when the Giants finished eighth. By his third season, they won the pennant, and the right to play in the World Series—which McGraw refused to do.

The next season the Giants took the pennant again, and this time McGraw agreed to participate in the Series. His Giants defeated the Philadelphia Athletics, 4 games to 1, the first of three World Championships McGraw would win as manager. **TS**

**John McGraw**

## Nice Guys Sometimes Finish First

In the early 1900s, Pittsburgh's Honus Wagner was not only baseball's best player, but also one of its most popular. Despite his stocky appearance, and the fact that he was bow-legged, he had amazing physical gifts. Not only was he a great hitter. He always seemed to be among the National League leaders in steals, and he was the league's most adroit shortstop. Wagner was also an easy-going genial sort, well loved by his teammates and fans.

In the 1909 World Series, Wagner came up against the American League's premier player—Detroit's Ty Cobb. While perhaps as talented as Wagner, Cobb was not only not as popular, he was intensely disliked by many. A driven and often cruel player, Cobb could get under the skin of friends and foes alike. Yet, he dominated the American League as much as Wagner did the National. Cobb had just won his third straight

**Honus Wagner**

batting title, the 35-year old Wagner his fourth. Wagner was considered a human vacuum cleaner at shortstop. Cobb was a base-stealing expert. Wagner seemed averse to the attention his skills earned him. Cobb seemed to need it to chase away inner demons.

In what was becoming a dog-eat-dog world in baseball, Cobb appeared to have the clear edge. He viewed every game as a war, his opponents as mortal enemies. Wagner viewed baseball as just a game, a pleasant pastime, much like fishing. Going into the Series, many fans had predicted that "surely Cobb would eat him [Wagner] alive."

However, an interesting thing happened. Before the first game, Wagner wandered over to the Detroit dugout and introduced himself to Cobb. Surrounded by a bevy of photographers, Cobb seemed to have no choice but to chat amiably with Wagner. This wasn't a prelude to a war, it was a tea party.

Oh, Cobb could play this game, too. He could make nice with opponents and then, to get an edge, cheapshot them the first time their back was turned. But Wagner never seemed to give him the chance. There was a story that Cobb had called Wagner a krauthead and tried to take him out on a slide into second, but both players later denied it. Cobb would later say there was no way he'd take on a man of Wagner's size and strength.

Whatever happened, Wagner not only never became intimidated, he never lost his poise. He batted .333 during the Series and stole six bases. In the field, he was flawless.

On the other hand, for whatever the reason, Cobb clearly wasn't on top of his game. After batting .377 during the regular season, he batted just .231, getting just 1 hit in his final 11 at bats. Without Cobb at his best, the Tigers couldn't keep pace with Pittsburgh and eventually lost the Series, four games to three. In one sense, it was to be the peak of both men's careers. Although Wagner played for 7 more years, and Cobb for another 19, neither player would ever reach another World Series. **TS**

# The Wild, Wild Ways of Rube Waddell

**B**efore there were "Flakes," there were "Rubes." If Philadelphia A's manager Connie Mack hadn't known it before he took the train to Punxsatawney, Pa. to pick up his latest pitching prospect, then he surely knew soon after, that no one was more appropriately named than Rube Waddell.

Standing 6-1, 196-pounds, the kid had a fastball that would light up today's speed guns and a curve ball with a sharp enough break to keep hitters jumping out of the batter's box. From 1902 to 1905, he would be the most dominant left-handed pitcher in baseball, winning more than 20-games in four straight seasons with the A's. However, as Mack would later say, "he had a million-dollar body and a 10-cent mind."

The flakiness would keep Waddell from having success in the major leagues in his first three seasons. He had a drinking problem, a love of fishing, which often took priority over baseball, and a strange fascination with fires. Throughout his career, if a fire truck drove by the ballpark with its sirens blazing, Waddell had to be restrained to keep him from following it—whether or not he was pitching.

Mack had heard all those stories before he began recruiting Waddell in 1902. After Waddell had been released by Chicago, Mack telegraphed him several times, offering him a contract, but never getting an answer. Mack was ready to give up when he finally received a short, terse reply: "Come and get me!"

After finding Waddell in Punxsatawney, Mack had little problem in talking him into coming to Philadelphia—with one slight hitch. On the way to the train station, Waddell made Mack stop at one store, and then another, and then another. He was getting Mack to pay off his debts.

When they finally arrived at the train station, they were met by a group of rather menacing looking men. Mack was feeling rather nervous, having exhausted his cash supply along the way. Then, one of the men stepped forward and offered his hand. "Thank you for taking (Waddell) out of town," the man said.

That was the first day of a lot of long days Mack had to spend baby-sitting Waddell. There were times when Mack had private investigators watching Waddell's every move, other times when Mack withheld part of Waddell's pay so he wouldn't spend it on alcohol. Then there was the time Mack paid off a man to pretend he had been viciously beaten by Waddell in one of the many bar brawls Waddell had problems remembering. That shamed Waddell into staying sober, at least for a short while.

After six seasons of putting up with the eccentric Waddell, Mack and the rest of the team could no longer stomach his bizarre behavior. The star pitcher was released after the 1907 season, a season in which he still won 19 games and led the league in strikeouts. Waddell then signed with St. Louis, where he had two good seasons; however, by 1910 he was out of baseball.

Yet, even in his shortened career, Waddell won 191 games, threw 50 shutouts, and struck out more than 2,300 batters—statistics good enough to get him into the Hall of Fame in 1946. Unfortunately, Waddell's wild ways shortened his life as well as his career. He died of tuberculosis in 1914, at the age of 37. **TS**

# Christy's Triple Shutout World Series

It should have been an easy decision for New York Giants' manager John McGraw. His star pitcher, Christy Mathewson, had been nothing short of spectacular in this, the 1905 World Series. He had pitched two complete game shutouts against the Philadelphia A's. He had allowed just eight hits and struck out 14. Now, with the teams heading into game five, the logical thing for McGraw to do was to rest Mathewson. After all, the Giants led the best of seven series three games to one. Mathewson had just pitched game three, which meant if he pitched game five, it would be on just one day's rest.

However, the amount of rest Mathewson needed was a tricky question. If Mathewson didn't pitch until game six, he'd be pitching on three days rest. When he was that rested, he had problems controlling his bread-and-butter

**Christy Mathewson**

pitch—the fadeaway, or screwball.

McGraw looked into Mathewson's eyes and asked him what he thought. "I'd like to pitch," Mathewson said. "I feel fine."

From the day McGraw had taken the job with the Giants, to the day Mathewson retired, McGraw put his faith in the man they called "the Christian Gentleman."

It might have been natural for McGraw to mistrust Mathewson, since the two men were so very different. Mathewson was a tall, good-looking man, noted for his easy-going personality and clean living. McGraw was stocky, had a big nose, and a penchant for drinking, swearing, and fighting.

However, he also believed in Mathewson. Before McGraw had arrived in 1904, the Giants had toyed with playing Mathewson at other positions. Not McGraw. Playing Mathewson anywhere else was just downright stupid, McGraw said. Mathewson would reward him by not winning less than 20 games for 12 straight seasons. He would win 30 or more games four times.

So when Mathewson said he felt fine, McGraw sent him to the mound. This time, however, it wasn't so easy. In four of the first five innings, Philadelphia put runners on. Each time, though, Mathewson bore down and kept them from scoring. In the bottom of the fifth, the Giants scored on a sacrifice fly, but in the top of the sixth the overflow crowd at the Polo Grounds wondered if that would be enough.

Fred Hartsel led off with a single, and then was forced out on Briscoe Lord's grounder. Up came Harry Davis, who had led the league in RBIs. If the A's were going to break through, now was the time. But Davis didn't get the chance. Catcher Roger Bresnahan caught Lord off first base and threw him out. With two down, Davis singled. Then Lave Cross grounded out to end the inning and the threat.

From there, Mathewson only seemed to get stronger, as he retired the last nine men in order. Mathewson had pitched 27 consecutive scoreless innings, three complete game shutouts, still a World Series record.

Grantland Rice, who would go on to become one of the nation's most famous sports reporters, would write: "In those few days he was the greatest pitcher I've ever seen. I believe he could have continued to pitch shutouts until Christmas." **TS**

# The Consummate Hitter

For once in his life, Ty Cobb wasn't sure whether baseball was the right thing for him.

It was 1903 and Cobb was just two years away from starting one of the greatest major league careers in history. However, all he knew at that moment was that he had been cut from a minor-league team. He needed to call home and tell his father. He expected his father would tell him to come home. But, to his surprise, W.H. Cobb told him quite the opposite.

Earlier that year, Cobb had left home at the age of 17 to pursue a career in baseball. His parents had been dead set against it. The night before he was to leave, he was up until 3 a.m. arguing the point with his father. Finally, probably figuring Ty would bolt on his own accord, his father gave him his blessing. "You've chosen. So be it, son," he said. "Go get it out of your system, and let us hear from you."

Cobb made the team—barely—when one of the veteran players sat out over a contract dispute. However, when that player came back two games into the season, Cobb was released. He was crushed and angry, feeling that this was his only shot at playing baseball professionally.

One of his teammates, who had also been released, was on his way to try out for a semi-pro team in Alabama. He told Cobb that team was also looking for an outfielder and that he should come along. But Cobb was so distraught he was ready to throw in the towel on a baseball career and go home. He telephoned his father to tell him the news, fully expecting that he would agree. Instead, he heard something quite different.

"Go after it," Cobb's father said after Ty told him about the semi-pro opportunity. "And I want to tell you one other thing—don't come home a failure."

Although that conversation left Ty shaking, it also filled him with resolve. He not only made the team and the starting lineup, he soon contended for a league batting title. Later that season he was recalled to the minors. The season after that he was sold to the major league Detroit Tigers.

Cobb went on to play professionally for 24 years, and many people claimed he was the greatest player who ever lived. He was the consummate hitter—winning a record 12 batting titles—a batter who could spot the third baseman playing back on the fringe of the outfield and then lay down a perfect bunt. Or see a shortstop cheating toward second and slap the ball into the area he'd just vacated.

He was an ultra-aggressive base runner, who would, on occasion, boldly declare to a shortstop he was on his way to steal second base and then come in sliding with his spikes high.

Cobb was the ultimate competitor, a man who viewed each game as a war. And it was this attitude that made him one of the most disliked players in the game. However, many people knew that Cobb's fierceness—and meanness—could be attributed to what happened in his personal life.

Despite the huge influence he exerted on his son, Cobb's father never got a chance to see him play a major-league game. One night, his wife mistook him for a burglar, and shot and killed him. Ty's friends said he never got over it. They also noticed a difference in the way he played, suddenly with reckless abandon, and unyielding aggressiveness.

"After the shooting, I figure that much of what he did on the diamond was for (his father)," Cobb's childhood companion Joe Cunningham said. "Seemed he was out to pay tribute to him in death. The thing is, his father opposed his playing ball, but he cared enough to let Ty go and prove he was a man. Ty owed him for that, and he never stopped paying him back." **TS**

# One Last Moment of Glory for a Bitter Hero

Grover Cleveland Alexander sat in the bullpen, dozing. The day before he had won game six of the 1926 World Series; he knew that unless there was an emergency, he wouldn't be needed for game seven. So he dozed, perhaps sleeping off a hangover, perhaps reflecting on a career in which he would eventually win 373 games over 20 seasons.

Alexander hadn't lived a charmed life. In fact, his life in baseball seemed filled with pitfalls from the very beginning. In his first season of pro ball, an errant throw by a shortstop hit him smack between the eyes when he tried to break up a double play. Alexander lapsed into a coma for two days and when he came out of it, he had double vision.

After two months the double vision cleared, and the next year he was back in baseball. Two years later he was in the major leagues, although he would continue to be plagued by epileptic seizures for the rest of his life.

For the next seven seasons he was the cornerstone of the Philadelphia Phillies, never winning fewer than 19 games, and winning 30 or more games in three consecutive seasons, from 1915 to 1917.

However, at the same time, World War I was raging in Europe. The Phillies, anticipating that Alexander would be drafted, traded him to Chicago in 1918. Shortly after that, Alexander was sent to France. When he returned, he was a different man. His hearing had been severely damaged by the shelling, and his drinking—he was, like his father and grandfather before him, an alcoholic—had gotten worse.

Still, he had several successful seasons for the Cubs, winning 27 games in 1920 and 22 games in 1923. The Cubs, though, tired of his drinking and his prickliness, and they waived him in 1926. At 39 years old, it appeared he was through.

However, he was reborn when the St. Louis Cardinals signed him for $4,000. He won nine games down the stretch to help the Cards advance to the World Series against Babe Ruth and the New York Yankees.

Now, in game seven, Alexander was broken out of his reverie by player-manager Rogers Hornsby. He'd decided to call upon the aging pitcher to get the Cards out of a tight jam in the seventh inning.

"We're ahead 3-2, but the Yankees have the bases loaded and there are two out," Hornsby told him, looking into his eyes to make sure Alexander was up to the task. Alexander just grabbed the ball and took the mound.

The hitter was Tony Lazzeri, a rookie who had driven in more than 100 runs that season. On the first pitch, Alexander fooled him with a curve that dropped in for a strike. Then Lazzeri ripped the next pitch down the left field line, but it curved just foul. Alexander noted later that if that ball had been hit just a foot or two more to

**Grover Cleveland Alexander**

the right, he wouldn't have been a hero, he would have been "just an old bum."

Lazzeri took a mighty cut at Alexander's next pitch, but missed, and the Yankees' threat was turned back. Alexander shut them out the rest of the way to clinch the series. For Alexander, it was a sweet way to end a tough season. He'd won two games in the Series as a starter, and had saved the final game with brilliant relief.

Still, it didn't seem to quell a deep bitterness he appeared to have inside from the alcoholism and obstacles he'd encountered in life.

"How'd it feel to strike out Lazzeri?" a reporter asked in the clubhouse.

"Go ask Lazzeri how it felt," Alexander snapped, as he walked away. **TS**

## The Long Wait for a Championship

Walter Johnson sat in the bullpen, feeling the disappointment growing within him with each passing inning. It was game seven of the 1924 World Series, and the New York Giants had a 3-1 lead over Johnson's Washington Senators in the eighth inning

For years, Johnson's pitching had carried the Senators. He'd won 25 games or more 7 straight seasons, and led the league in strikeouts 8 consecutive years. He would finish his career with 417 wins, second only to Cy Young. However, for all his greatness, Johnson had never pitched in a World Series—until now. Washington had never had enough talented players around him to win a pennant, until 1924.

Now, sitting in the bullpen, Johnson had to wrestle with the knowledge that in his first and perhaps only chance to win a world championship, he had fallen on his face. He had lost game one when he gave up two home runs and then a bases-loaded single in the 12th. He had lost game five, in part, by making a base running mistake and an error.

Now, in game seven, the Senators were on the brink of losing the whole Series. Only that was about to change. In the bottom of eighth, Washington had men on first and second with one out. Senators' player-manager Bucky Harris handed Johnson the ball and told him to warm up. The crowd went crazy, erupting in such a cheer that even the Giants' pitcher seemed to be shaken. He walked the next batter on four straight pitches to load the bases. One out later, Harris hit a sharp single down the third base line to drive in two runs. Although the next batter grounded out to end the inning, there was hope in Washington. The Senators had tied the game and Walter Johnson was on the mound.

Although he'd had another brilliant season—winning 23 games and leading the league in ERA and strikeouts—at 36-years old, Johnson's stamina seemed diminished. And this was becoming painfully apparent, even to the adoring Washington crowd. In the ninth, Johnson enticed the first batter into a popout, but then Frankie Frisch tripled to right center. Johnson walked the next batter and the crowd held its collective breath.

However, Johnson was not going to blow a third opportunity. He bore down and cranked up his fastball. It popped into the catcher's mitt carrying nearly the same force it had 16-years earlier when Johnson had broken into the big leagues. The next Giants' batter struck out, and the following hitter grounded out. Johnson was out of the jam.

For the next three innings the Giants put men on base against Johnson, but they couldn't break through. Each time Johnson needed a strikeout, he reached back and threw overpowering heat.

In the bottom of the twelfth, the Giants

recorded two quick outs and nearly ended the inning when Muddy Ruel popped up. But the Giants catcher dropped the ball to give Ruel new life. Ruel doubled, bringing Johnson to the plate. He hit a hard grounder, the shortstop fumbled it, and Johnson was safe at first, with Ruel going to third. Earl McNeely then smacked a grounder that seemed destined to be the third out—until it hit a pebble and bounced over Freddie Lindstrom's head at third. Ruel crossed the plate with the winning run. Walter Johnson and the Senators finally had a World Championship. **TS**

# The Clown Who Was a Baseball Genius

It was a boneheaded move, just the kind of maneuver the critics might have predicted when the New York Yankees hired Casey Stengel as their manager for the 1949 season. Now, with the pennant on the line, he was going to his best relief pitcher in the *third* inning of a game. The Yankees were behind 2-0 to the Boston Red Sox, there was one out, and the bases were loaded. The logical move would have been to bring in a long reliever, or someone just to get them out of the inning with minimal damage. To bring in his "stopper" now was too much of a gamble. After all, if the game remained close, who would Stengel go to in the late innings?

Before coming to the Yankees, Stengel had managed for nine years in the major leagues, and none of his teams had finished in the top half of the league standings. He had been fired twice, and when the Yankees tapped him, he was managing the minor-league Oakland Oaks. He had a reputation as a bit of clown, a man who had a way of twisting the language into something that sounded great, but often didn't make any sense. He was a showman, who loved talking to writers and, when in the right mood, would do anything photographers asked. His behavior was a stark contrast to the austere, businesslike manner of Yankee managers of the past. Some sportswriters implied that Stengel's being hired to manage the Yankees was nothing but a joke.

Even the Yankees players were scratching their heads when they heard Stengel had been hired. And no one was reassured, when in his first press conference, Stengel

**Casey Stengel**

called the Yankees' owner by the wrong first name and said he didn't know Joe DiMaggio.

However, during the 1949 season Stengel had shown a unique ability to succeed despite obstacles. He had done an admirable job of rotating players to cover up for injuries, and taking advantage of limited talent. And he had kept the Yankees in first place most of the season. But now, at the end, the Yankees were struggling to hold on.

Boston, managed by former Yankees' manager Joe McCarthy, had rallied to take the league lead late in the season. Now it was all boiling down to a two-game series. The Yankees needed to sweep the series to win the title, but they were behind in game one and looking vulnerable. Stengel's move was looking like a blunder. His stopper Joe Page walked the first batter, forcing in a run, and then walked the next batter. It was 4-0. But Stengel stuck with Page, and he rewarded him by getting out of the inning. In the next two innings, the Yankees slowly but surely tied the score.

Then Page just seemed to get stronger. He shut out the Sox the rest of the way, giving up just one hit. In the eighth inning the Yankees took the lead for good. They wound up with a win and a tie for first. The next day they won again, winning the pennant.

The Yankees would go on and win the World Series that year, and then under Stengel's helm, repeat the accomplishment for the next four seasons—an unprecedented five consecutive world championships. By the time Stengel left the Yankees after the 1960 season, his teams had won ten pennants and seven World Series. In the end, the only joke involving Casey Stengel was the one the Yankees played on the other American League teams they dominated for nearly his entire time as manager. **TS**

# The Dazzling Old Rookie

I f there was one thing Dazzy Vance had come to learn in his long wait to make the big leagues, it was that opportunities come and go. . . and then come again.

Heck, how else to explain that at age 31, he was a rookie in the majors? Sure, there had been opportunities to move up to the big time before, a cup of coffee with the New York Yankees and Pittsburgh Pirates in 1915, another short stint with the Yankees in 1917, but Vance had never measured up. It wasn't until 1922 that he came up for good. And even then the call up was tainted. When the Brooklyn Robins purchased catcher Hank DeBerry from a minor league team in New Orleans, the team made them take Vance as well. The Robins never regretted it. Vance won 18 games in each of his first two seasons, then went 28-6 in 1924 and was named the league's Most Valuable Player. He had gone from being a pitcher nobody wanted, to the most dominant pitcher in the league.

With that in mind, it was no surprise that when Vance just missed throwing a no-hitter against Philadelphia in 1925 (he gave up just one hit), he wasn't frustrated or disappointed. In fact, when he took the mound five days later, again against the Phillies, Philadelphia manager Art Fletcher yelled at him, "Well, you lucky stiff, you'll get no one-hitter today!"

"I wouldn't be too sure about that, Art," Vance yelled back. "With these humpty-dumpties you've got, anything can happen."

Vance had every reason to be confident. He had a tremendous fastball that was powered by his long arms—he had an 83-inch reach. "He could throw a creampuff through a battleship," a player once said.

However, Vance didn't just rely on his natural talent, he used a little bit of guile learned from years of bouncing around the minor leagues. He took to wearing a long-sleeved white shirt under his jersey. Those sleeves would flutter in the summer breezes, often distracting the batter. Baseball would eventually make such shirts illegal. On this day, though, there were no holds barred for Vance.

In the second inning, the Phillies broke through with an unearned run. Nelson Hawks, the same man who had broken up Vance's no-hitter five days before, hit a fly ball to left field. Jimmy Johnston, normally an infielder, but today playing left, botched the catch and Hawks wound up on third base. He then scored on a sacrifice fly.

That kind of sequence might unnerve a young pitcher, but not Vance. He continued to pitch confidently and comfortably, in the end walking just one, striking out nine—and not allowing a hit. At the same time, the Robins' offense came through for him, scoring 10 runs. By the time Vance reached the ninth, he could smell a no-hitter. But with two outs, Fred Leach smashed a Vance pitch into left field. For a moment it looked as if it would drop—but at the last moment, Johnston raced over and snatched it out of the air. Vance had his no-hitter.

Vance would go on to pitch for 10 more years, winning a total of 197 games and striking out more than 2,000 hitters in his career. Not too bad for a pitcher who didn't even make it to the majors until he was past 30 years old. **TS**

# The Babe Calls His Shot

For the first time in a long time, Babe Ruth wasn't the best player in the league. Oh sure, in 1932 he was still near the top of his game, finishing second in the league in home runs with 41, hitting .341, and knocking in 137 runs. But he wasn't the best player in the league. Heck, he wasn't even clearly the best player on the Yankees. He had stiff competition from Lou Gehrig, who had batted .349 and had 151 RBIs.

Yet much of the focus of the World Series between the Yankees and the Chicago Cubs was on Babe Ruth, and he would have it no other way. Besides being the most dominating player of his time, Ruth was also the consummate showman. Other players might hit more homers, but they didn't hit them as far. Others might drive in more runs, but they didn't do them in as many dramatic situations as Ruth.

Now, in what would turn out to be his last World Series, Ruth was determined to make a stir. He started it with his mouth. He called the Cubs cheapskates for not voting full World Series shares to players who had joined the team late in the season. The Cubs returned with taunts at Ruth, calling him old and washed up.

The war of words caught the public's attention. After the Yankees won the first two games of the Series in New York, they traveled to Chicago for game three. It took a police escort to get the Yankees to their hotel, and on entering the building, Ruth and his wife were spat on.

For game three, Wrigley Field was filled to over capacity, as nearly 50,000 fans filled the park.

After trailing early, the Cubs rallied to tie the game at 4–4 in the fourth inning. Emotions ran high as Ruth stepped up in the fifth. The boos were deafening, and many of the Cubs moved from their seats in the dugout to the top step to scream insults at him.

Ruth had already hit a three-run homer in

**A painting depicts Ruth "calling" his homer**

over at the Cubs and raised a finger on his right hand. Some said he was pointing to where he was going to hit the ball out, others said he was just noting there was a strike against him, and jeering the Cubs.

Ruth watched the next three pitches go by. Two of them were balls, the other one a strike. Ruth held up two fingers. Later, Cubs catcher Gabby Hartnett would report that Ruth said, "It only takes one to hit."

The next pitch was a changeup curve and Ruth jumped all over it, driving it deep into center field, the longest home run hit in Wrigley Field. It gave the Yankees a 5-4 lead, and helped propel them to their third straight Series victory.

the first to give the Yanks an early lead. Now he stepped into the batter's box with a smile on his face. If he was anything but amused, he didn't show it. He took a called strike. Then he looked

In the clubhouse afterward, Ruth was in his element. "Did Mr. Ruth chase those guys back into the dugout?" he yelled to no one in particular. "Mr. Ruth sure did."

The next morning, at least one New York newspaper had a headline that virtually screamed about Ruth's "called shot," even though Ruth hadn't confirmed or denied it.

The Yankees would win the fourth game and finish with a Series sweep. Lou Gehrig had been just about unstoppable in the Series, hitting three homers, driving in nine runs and batting .529. But it was Ruth, and his called shot, that seemed to overshadow everything and everyone else—just as he did almost every day he ever stepped onto a baseball field. **TS**

# The Toughest Player-Manager

It was the bottom of the 11th inning. The Chicago Cubs trailed the Boston Braves by three runs, but the Cubs had the bases loaded with two out. Rollie Hemsley, their light-hitting catcher was due up, but manager Rogers Hornsby was looking for a pinch-hitter. He picked himself.

Hornsby knew he would be second-guessed; that season of 1932 had been all about second-guessing. Heck, even the home crowd was grumbling when he stepped up to the plate. He was 36-years old, and had virtually retired from playing. He suffered from bone spurs in his heels and other injuries that limited his mobility.

On the other hand, for more than 15 years, he had been the best hitter in the National League. He'd won six straight batting titles, and batted over .400 three times, including 1924, when hit .424. In the 16 seasons he played 100 games or more, he hit less than .300 only once.

So Hornsby took a trip to the plate. He worked the count to 3-and-2, and then parked a fastball in the stands for the win. It was a sweet feeling for Hornsby, until he returned to the dugout and found a note from team president Bill Veeck. Hornsby had been summoned to Veeck's office.

For all his talent and accomplishments, Hornsby was not a well-liked man, especially as a player-manager. He was demanding, humorless, and blunt to a fault. He regularly told off management. He would spout off to the press about certain players' shortcomings, and then discipline them for petty offenses, such as eating in the dugout. "I wanted to be a success at playing ball," he would write later. "I didn't want to tell funny stories, or brag back and forth."

However, if Hornsby was tough on players and management, he was even tougher on himself. He didn't go to movies because he felt it would hurt his eyes. When his mother died just before the 1926 World Series, he postponed the funeral until after the Series. He had driven himself to become one of the best hitters of all time, and when the situation was right, he could drive a team to greatness, as he did when he played and managed the St. Louis Cardinals to the 1926 world championship. Hornsby was an intense competitor who believed there was only one right way to win—his way.

So later that day, when Veeck questioned his judgment, implying that had Hornsby struck out he would have alienated the crowd and the team, Hornsby barked back.

"I don't manage scared. I play the best man I can possibly get in the best spot."

Veeck backed down that time, but later that season he fired Hornsby, even though the Cubs were in first place at the time. For Hornsby it was a relief. If he couldn't manage and win his way, he didn't want to manage at all. **TS**

# The Angry Winner

**P**hiladelphia A's pitcher Lefty Grove could feel the anger building in his chest as he watched the ball heading to the outfield. It was going right to the rookie, the one who was playing because veteran Al Simmons had left the team for a few days.

The ball was going to be trouble, and Grove knew it. He was trying to win his 17th game in a row, a major league record. But as he watched this ball heading to the outfield, he had the feeling the rookie was going to blow his chance. If that happened, Grove was going to make sure there was hell to pay.

It was 1931 and Robert Moses "Lefty" Grove was on his way to becoming the American League's first Most Valuable Player. He would go 31-4 that season, and lead the league in ERA and strikeouts. In the two previous seasons he had won 48 games, and helped lead the A's to two World Series championships. But despite all his success, Grove wasn't a peaceful man.

"Lose a 1-0 game and you didn't want to get into the clubhouse with Grove and (Mickey) Cochrane," one teammate would say. "You'd be ducking stools and gloves and bats and whatever else would fly."

Grove just refused to settle for second best. When he turned to baseball for a living, he found frustrations. Some of his best years were spent pitching for Baltimore in the International League. The Baltimore franchise wasn't affiliated with a major league club, so it didn't need to move Grove along to the big leagues. It held on to its star until Philadelphia's Connie Mack coughed up $100,600 for him, the most ever paid for a minor league player.

However, the frustration and anger wasn't over once he reached the big leagues. For two years Grove battled with his control before finally settling down and winning 20 games in 1927.

Now, in 1931 he was in the midst of his greatest run. It was August and Grove had tied a

**Lefty Grove**

major league record by winning 16 straight games. A win over the lowly St. Louis Browns would give him the record, and it seemed a dead-cinch lock. Only the A's weren't cooperating. They were being shut out, and now Grove watched as the rookie misplayed the fly ball and then dropped it, costing his team a run that would be the difference.

The A's eventually lost 1-0, and Grove went a little crazy. Oh, he had thrown fits before, but this was something else. He tried to tear his locker door off its hinges, and when he couldn't do that, he kicked it until it splintered. He also pulled off his uniform and tore it up.

He didn't talk to anyone for a

week after that—except Al Simmons. "It was Simmons' fault," Grove recalled years later. "And I told him about it."

Grove didn't get the consecutive game record, but he evidently got over his anger. He pitched another ten years, and controlled his temper well enough to win a total of 300 games in his career. **TS**

## A Sad End to a Great Career

**M**ickey Cochrane put his hand up, a reflex action to protect his face. It didn't help. There was only the dull thud of the baseball striking his skull, and then darkness for ten long days.

Cochrane was one of the most talented catchers baseball had ever known. A 12-year veteran, at age 34 he had already played on three pennant winning and two world championship teams in Philadelphia, and played and managed two pennant winners and a world championship team in Detroit. Sure, the past few seasons had been tough on him; there were whispers he had become a real liability as a defensive catcher, and then there had been the illness. In 1936, he had a nervous breakdown, and was forced to take a leave of absence from the Tigers. He missed most of the season that year, but this year, in 1937, Cochrane was back with a vengeance. He was hitting .306.

Cochrane could always hit. In 1925, as a rookie with the Philadelphia A's, he hit .331. From 1929 to 1931, while the A's were dominating the American League, he batted .346. He had outstanding speed, especially for a catcher; sometimes he even hit lead off, although he was accustomed to batting third. Oh, and he had a mind for baseball. When Philadelphia's manager and owner Connie Mack put Cochrane and teammate Lefty Grove up for sale, the Tigers went for Cochrane, because of his talent and also because they had confidence Cochrane could also manage the team. He didn't disappoint them, leading the Tigers to two pennants and a world championship in his first two seasons.

Part of Cochrane's success was his competitive fire, but it could also be his undoing. The Gashouse Gang of the St. Louis Cardinals were especially adept at throwing Cochrane off his game with their insults. Pepper Martin seemed to steal bases at will, and some Tigers' pitchers blamed it on Cochrane's poor throwing arm.

Cochrane's nickname became "Black Mike" for his tantrums after close losses. In the 1934 World Series against the Cardinals, Cochrane checked himself into hospitals to get his rest. It didn't work as the Tigers lost.

However, in 1937, he seemed to be on his way back. When he stepped to the plate on May 15 against the New York Yankees he was hitting .306. Then Bump Hadley's live fastball struck Cochrane's head so hard it just about bounced all the way back to the pitcher's mound. Cochrane landed, unconscious, face down at the plate. For four days he was listed in critical condition with a triple skull fracture. After ten days, he finally regained consciousness.

Cochrane would later return to manage the Tigers, but he was barred from playing by the team owner. A little more than a year after the beaning, Cochrane was fired. It had been just three seasons since he had managed the team to a world championship. It was a sad end to a great, but troubled career. **TS**

# The Iron Horse

It was a routine ground ball between first base and the pitcher's mound. Yankee pitcher Johnny Murphy scrambled after it, scooped it up, and prepared to throw. But he had to wait for a few seconds for Lou Gehrig to move over and cover the bag. As the other Yankees' players watched the play unfold, they sensed something was terribly wrong.

Gehrig had been the hub of the Yankees. A big, swarthy home run hitter who had played in a major league record 2,122 consecutive games, he was nicknamed the Iron Horse. However, the man who had driven in nearly 2,000 runs and had more than 2,500 hits seemed to be losing it, and losing it very suddenly.

Sure, he was coming off a down season, at least by his standards. In 1938 he had batted "only" .295 and driven in 114 runs. In the off-season he went to see a doctor who told him he was suffering from a gall bladder condition.

Gehrig changed his diet. That winter he spent a lot of time ice skating to stay in shape. He knew he was getting older, but only two seasons before, he had hit .351 and driven in 138 runs. If he could just stay healthy, he reasoned, he still had a lot of great years ahead. Yet, when he started spring training in 1939 it was like he'd aged 10 years. His swing was slow and awkward and lacked the power of even the season before.

Gehrig shrugged it off. He always had problems in spring training, he said. It was just a matter of time before he came around. Everyone else, from his teammates to his fans to team management, was beginning to wonder. One afternoon, Joe DiMaggio had watched Gehrig miss 12 straight pitches during batting practice. "They were all fastballs too, the kind of pitch that Lou would normally hit into the next county," DiMaggio said.

The Yankees were also starting to fear for Gehrig's safety. He had never been a very graceful fielder, but he was becoming even slower and

**Lou Gehrig**

clumsier. Teammates feared that one day he wouldn't be able to get his glove up fast enough to protect his face.

Yet manager Joe McCarthy was hesitant to pull Gehrig out of the lineup. He felt when it was time, Gehrig himself would pull the plug. As spring training wound down, though, there was a flicker of hope that Gehrig would return to his former self. In an exhibition game against the Brooklyn Dodgers,

Gehrig had four hits, two of them homers. That game insured Gehrig would be the Yankees starting first baseman on opening day.

That exhibition game turned out to be just an aberration, though. In the fifth inning of the season opener against Boston, the Yankees had a runner on third with Joe DiMaggio due up. In the past, the Red Sox would have gone after DiMaggio, not wanting to face Gehrig, who was up next, with men on base. But now, it was different. The Red Sox opted to walk DiMaggio to pitch to Gehrig. It was a cold slap in the face for Gehrig, but what made it worse, was he hit into a double play.

For six more games Gehrig struggled on this way, until a game against the Washington Senators. It was the ninth inning when the routine ground ball was hit between first and the pitcher's mound. Pitcher Johnny Murphy fielded it, hesitated, and then threw to Gehrig for the out. As they ran off the field, Murphy gave Gehrig a hearty congratulation. Gehrig just shook his head. He knew he had made the play closer than it should have been. He realized his teammates and fans were just thankful he could make routine plays.

Following the next game, Gehrig told McCarthy he needed a day off. The consecutive playing streak ended at 2,130. Gehrig would never play in the major leagues again.

A month later he was diagnosed with amyotrophic lateral sclerosis (ALS), a rare and incurable disease. That summer he would retire from baseball, giving his famous farewell speech in which he would declare, "I consider myself the luckiest man on the face of the earth."

Two years later, he would pass away in his sleep. Since that time, ALS has been commonly referred to as Lou Gehrig's disease. **TS**

## "King Carl" Shines Among the All-Stars

The pitcher had just walked Heinie Manush to put runners on first and second with none out. Standing on the mound, he watched Babe Ruth step into the batter's box. The pitcher knew it didn't get any easier after Ruth—waiting on deck was Lou Gehrig, and stirring in the dugout was Jimmie Foxx.

In this, the 1934 All-Star game, New York Giants' pitcher Carl Hubbell couldn't afford the luxury of remembering how Ty Cobb had warned him six years before, telling him that throwing the screwball was going to ruin his arm. Then, and now, he had had to make a decision. He was going to live and die with the screwball, and the heck with the consequences.

Ruth was anxious to take his cuts. The season before he had hit the first home run in the first All-Star game. But now as he stood at the plate, he only watched as the man with the deformed arm fired three pitches, each of which broke away from him. Ruth struck out, and went back to the dugout, as one newspaper account of the day put it, "looking decidedly puzzled."

The screwball was a wicked pitch, one that required the pitcher to snap his wrist on release, facing his palm away from him. That resulted in a kind of reverse curve, and it also put undue strain on the arm. When Hubbell's arm dangled at his side, it looked deformed.

Gehrig was not one to be distracted by the odd appearance of Hubbell's arm. He would go on to win the Triple Crown that season—lead the league in average, home runs, and RBIs—and only strike out 31 times. He was determined not to let the pitches go by untouched.

Yet, he too struck out, swinging at a low screwball. As he walked back to the dugout he told Foxx, "You might as well cut. It won't get any higher."

Hubbell's success shouldn't really have been a surprise to anyone paying attention to the

National League. After coming up with the New York Giants in 1928, he would never have a losing season. Beginning in 1933, he'd win 20 or more games for five straight seasons. In 1933, he had thrown two complete game shutouts in the World Series against the Washington Senators, and been named the National League's Most Valuable Player.

What also frustrated hitters was Hubbell's remarkable control. He rarely got into trouble. In an 18-inning complete game shutout against St. Louis in 1933, he hadn't walked a batter. Over one stretch of that season, he strung together 46 straight scoreless innings, a National League record that would stand for 35 years.

Now with two out in the All-Star Game, Jimmie Foxx was the next challenge. A feared slugger, he had led the league in home runs and RBIs the two previous seasons. But Hubbell got him swinging and the National League was out of a jam.

In the second inning, Hubbell struck out Al Simmons and Joe Cronin, before Bill Dickey finally snapped the string with a single. Then Hubbell ended the inning by striking out pitcher Lefty Gomez.

In 1936 "King Carl" would again be named the league's MVP. From the end of the 1936 season through part of 1937, Hubbell would win 24 straight games, and wind up with a total of 253 victories in his career.

Still, perhaps the highlight of Hubbell's career was the 1934 All-Star game, when he struck out Ruth, Gehrig, Foxx, Simmons, and Cronin—five future Hall of Famers—all in a row. **TS**

## Satchel Paige's Big Moment

It wasn't a long walk from the Cleveland Indians' bullpen to the pitching mound, but it was slow one for Satchel Paige. He wanted to enjoy every step.

On this afternoon of July 9, 1948, Satchel Paige had finally gotten his call to pitch in a major-league game. He was 42 years-old, or at least claimed to be; some people said he looked 49. Having pitched in more than 2,500 games, Paige was beginning to believe this moment would never come.

Satchel Paige had been one of the biggest names in baseball. People referred to his 1-0 victory over Dizzy Dean years before in an exhibition game with a certain reverence. Over the years, millions of fans paid their way through the turnstiles to see him pitch. They had delighted in his antics, the way he would order all his fielders into the dugout, saying he didn't need them because opponents would never hit his pitches.

However, all his exploits had come in the Negro leagues, or foreign leagues, or exhibition games. He was shut out of major league baseball even though, time and again during exhibition games, he showed he could not only compete on that level, he could dominate.

Paige had watched as Jackie Robinson broke the color barrier in 1947. When people asked Paige if he was jealous, he would just shrug and say he could make more money in the Negro leagues and pitching exhibition games. Yet years later he would write about his true feelings.

"Signing Jackie like they did still hurt me deep down," Paige wrote in his autobiography. "I'd been the guy who'd started all that big talk about letting us in the big time. I'd been the one who everybody had said should be in the majors."

By 1948, though, Paige could see his opportunity. Larry Doby had broken the color line in the American League with Cleveland. Indians' owner Bill Veeck had shown a willingness to do anything to win and play to a full house.

So here was Paige, coming out of the bullpen. Veeck had been ridiculed for signing Paige. In his prime, 10 years before, he may have been able to pitch in the majors, but now it seemed he was too old. Veeck was treating him like a circus clown, the critics said. It was up to Paige to prove them wrong.

The first batter, Chuck Stevens, lined a single to left field. The second batter bunted Stevens to second. One of the most anticipated pitching debuts in history was getting off to a rocky start.

Paige struck out the next batter

**Satchel Paige**

for the second out. The next hitter flied out to end the inning. Paige was over the hump.

In the sixth, he gave up another hit, but he got out of the inning with a double play and a pop fly.

In Cleveland's half of the inning, Paige was lifted for a pinch-hitter—Larry Doby—but he had begun proving his point. That season, he would go 6-1 and pitch in the World Series, and, even though he was listed as 42-years old, he received some votes for Rookie of the Year.

Paige would continue pitching in and out of the majors for several more seasons, but never as well as 1948 when he finally proved he could pitch in the major leagues. **TS**

# The "Beast" Busts Up a World Series

It must have been a scary sight for any pitcher, looking down from the mound and seeing Jimmie Foxx, with his cutoff sleeves, flexing his enormous biceps. One pitcher said that even Foxx's hair seemed to have muscles.

However, to Burleigh Grimes, of the St. Louis Cardinals, who was preparing to pitch to the Philadelphia A's slugger in game five of the 1930 World Series, those muscles weren't as threatening. Grimes felt he had the key to beating the big man.

Foxx was an intimidating presence at 6 feet, 200 pounds. He had a robust body, held together with thick, heavy muscles. He was built, Foxx once said, from milking cows and painting barns.

New York Yankees' pitcher Lefty Gomez was one of those who wished Foxx had stayed on the farm. Gomez would tell the story of how he was having trouble seeing, so he bought a pair of glasses to wear while he pitched.

"One day my glasses fogged up while I was pitching," Gomez said. "Then when I cleaned them and looked at the plate and saw Foxx clearly, it frightened me so much I never wore them again."

In 1930, Foxx was in his third full season in the majors and just beginning to hit his prime; he would hit 58 homers in 1932, win the Triple Crown in 1933, and be named be the American League Most Valuable Player both years. But in 1930, he was "just" a power hitter with a propensity for striking out. He had hit 37 home runs, but had also led the league in strikeouts with 66.

Grimes felt that was the key. He had been pitching in the majors for more than 13 seasons, and he certainly knew how to set up a hitter. Because the rule banning spitballs had come down while Grimes was in the majors, he was allowed to continue throwing it, and it was a great weapon.

In game one of the Series, he had managed to get two of his spitters over for strikes against Foxx. Knowing that Foxx would be sitting on his spitball, Grimes took a risk and threw him a curve. Foxx struck out.

Now, in game five, Grimes remembered this as he stared in at Foxx. It was the ninth inning of a scoreless tie. There was one out and a runner on first. Any other pitcher would have been terrified of Foxx's power, but Grimes figured the way to beat the "Beast," as Foxx was nicknamed, was with brains. Grimes brought his hand to his mouth, and pretended to load up the ball with spit. Instead he got ready to throw a curve.

What Grimes hadn't anticipated was that this "Beast" had brains. . . and a long memory. Grimes had surprised Foxx the first time he threw him a curve; Foxx would later admit he didn't even realize Grimes *had* a curve. Grimes, in turn, would later confess he would throw just two curves in the entire series, both to Foxx. But this time when Grimes threw it, Foxx was ready. He hit it into the left field bleachers to give his team a 2-0 win.

Philadelphia would go on to win the series 4-2, and the "Beast" would go on intimidating pitchers for another 14 seasons. **TS**

# The Funniest Man in Baseball

**H**e was the funniest man in baseball, but on this day in 1937, all his New York Yankee teammates could feel for him was melancholy.

Vernon Louis "Lefty" Gomez was affectionately known as El Goofo to his teammates. He was a sportswriter's dream, regularly churning out witticisms that made for wonderful copy.

He owed his pitching success, he said, to "clean living and a fast outfield." Of home run hitter Jimmie Foxx he said, "He wasn't scouted, he was trapped." And of his RBI single in the 1933 All-Star game, the notoriously light hitting Gomez said, "I think 300 fans fainted in the stands when that ball fell in."

However, Gomez was more than a team cutup. During his career, he won more than 20 games five times and compiled a perfect 6-0 record in the five World Series in which he appeared. He had a first class fastball early in his career, and later developed a good curve and variety of off-speed pitches that allowed him to have continued success as he got older.

In 1937, however, he appeared to be on the downside of his career. After going 26-5 in 1934, he had struggled the next two seasons, going 12-15 and 13-7 with ERAs over 3.00. He was streaky early in the 1937 season, winning a few games in a row, then losing a few. In early August he had a 13-8 record, but hadn't won a game for nearly a month.

That's when he received word that his mother was ill. In between starts he packed up and went to California to be with her. After missing a turn in the rotation, he came back Aug. 13, and pitched in a loss. Clearly, he was drained by the 13-hour flight between coasts. His mother told him not to worry and stay back East for his next start. He did. An hour before he was scheduled to take the mound against Washington he received a telegram. His mother had passed away.

Gomez had never been known to take baseball too seriously. He would sometimes hold the ball between pitches just to watch a plane fly by. Yet on this day he seemed completely focused—he may have been emotionally devastated, but he was also determined. He went out and pitched a three-hit victory over Washington and then left for the funeral.

Gomez went on to win seven of his next eight decisions, three of them shutouts. He finished the season 21-11,

**Lefty Gomez**

with a league-leading 2.33 ERA. The Yankees would win the World Series with Gomez throwing a complete game victory in the deciding game.

Many of Gomez's contributions throughout his 14-year career couldn't be charted. He helped break in the young Joe DiMaggio—who joined the Yanks as a highly-touted rookie in 1936—with his special brand of humor.

One day with Gomez pitching, DiMaggio, playing a shallow center field, had to race back and make a last-second grab of a deep fly ball. When he came into the dugout, Gomez barked, "Hey, kid, why do you play so shallow out there?" DiMaggio responded, "I'm going to make them forget Speaker." [the great outfielder Tris Speaker, who always played a shallow center field] Gomez replied, "If you don't start playing deeper, you're going to make them forget *Gomez*."

Baseball fans knew there was never any chance of that. **TS**

# Master Melvin's Sweet Swing

**A**s he watched the ball flying majestically over the outfield fence, former New York Giants manager John McGraw had to think, "Thank God I didn't let anyone fool with my boy."

It was 1933, and Mel Ott had just hit what would turn out to be the game-winning, Series-clinching home run in the tenth-inning, allowing the Giants to defeat the Washington Senators and win the world championship. Ott's home run wasn't a shock, really, since by this time he had established himself as one of the best power hitters in the game; he'd go on to lead the National League in homers six times. But, had he not come under the tutelage of McGraw, someone might have changed that home run stroke.

In 1925, the 16-year old Ott had walked into then-manager McGraw's office, introduced himself, and asked for a tryout. After taking a quick glance at Ott, who was only 5-foot-9, McGraw's first instinct was probably to tell the boy to take a hike. However, the youngster had been recommended by one of McGraw's informal scouts, so he set him to work with a group of Giant rookies. What McGraw saw both appalled and amazed him. Ott had one of the most unorthodox swings he had ever seen. As the pitch approached, Ott, a left-handed hitter, would lift his right leg off the ground; then he'd bring it down as he swung. It looked as if he was stepping into a bucket.

For some reason, though, McGraw hesitated before rushing to correct so fundamental an error.

**Mel Ott**

McGraw noticed that while Ott's motion looked awkward, he was hitting everything thrown at him, and hitting it a long way. Ott's approach to the ball was strange, but his swing was beautiful, and McGraw was taken with it.

McGraw was known for taking certain players under his wing and Ott immediately became one of those. Ott had come to the Giants as a catcher, but McGraw immediately made him an outfielder. McGraw felt that crouching behind the plate would quickly wear out the thick-legged rookie.

At 16, Ott wasn't ready to play every day in the major leagues, but McGraw wasn't going to let him get away. In his first two seasons, Ott only occasionally left the bench to pinch-hit. The rest of the time was spent sitting next to McGraw and listening to him.

"He used to scare me sometimes," Ott would later say. "If some outfielder, either on our club or the opposition, played a ball badly or threw to the wrong base, he'd suddenly turn to me and yell, 'Don't let me ever catch you doing that.'"

During that first off-season, future Hall of Famer Casey Stengel, who was managing a minor league team at the time, asked McGraw if he wanted to send Ott to him for some more playing time and instruction. "The old man cussed me out and said that nobody was going to get his kid," Stengel recalled. "He was going to mold Master Melvin his way."

However, McGraw left Ott's swing alone. Ott was a dead pull hitter, perfectly built for the Polo Grounds and the short right field porch of 257 feet down the line. In 1928, Ott finally became a regular. In 1929, he hit 42 homers, knocked in 152 runs, and was on his way to dominating the league for the next several seasons.

In 1932, McGraw stepped down as manager for health reasons. His work with Ott was done. Never was that more evident then when his World Series-winning homer flew out of the park in 1933. **TS**

# Dizzy Dean's Endless Charm

As he left the hospital that October day in 1934, 'Ol Diz just knew that his life was charmed.

Jay Hanna "Dizzy" Dean had it all in 1934. He had won 30 games during the regular season. His bold pre-season prediction that he and his brother Paul "Daffy" Dean would win more than 40 games between them had come true when Paul won 19 games. Their team, the St. Louis Cardinals, had won the World Series, as the Dean brothers combined to win all four of the games. Dizzy Dean, star pitcher of the St. Louis Cardinals, was on top of the world.

Why, he'd even gotten reckless and had still come out smelling like a rose. That's why he was in the hospital that day.

In game four of the 1934 Series against the Detroit Tigers, Dean was inserted as a pinch-runner at first base. He broke for second on a ground ball, but forgot to slide and duck when the shortstop threw to first trying to complete the double play. Billy Rogell's throw hit Dean square in the forehead, knocking him to the ground. They carried Dean off the field on a stretcher and immediately rushed him to a hospital.

The public's concern for Dean's health went beyond what could be expected when an "average" player was seriously injured. Dean was one of the most beloved athletes in the country. Fans were in awe of his pitching ability, tickled by his "country bumpkin" sense of humor, and entertained by his showmanship. He was the leader of the "Gashouse Gang," as the Cardinals were nicknamed that season, the most eccentric of a group of off-beat players known as well for their personalities as their physical talent. With the country in the midst of a depression, people needed something more than just baseball to take their mind off the struggling economy. The Gashouse Gang helped do that.

Dean would talk long and loud with the

press, telling stories that often contradicted themselves ("Them ain't lies," he once explained, "them's scoops."). However, Dean was nobody's fool; rather, he was a master showman, not above creating a little drama to spice things up.

However, his being beaned in game four was no act. And when he emerged from the hospital, an anxious press corps awaited him.

"They X-rayed my head," he announced, "and didn't find anything!" Oh, there was a brain there, but luckily there was no injury. Dean had dodged a bullet, and indeed his life did seem charmed.

Yet, the reality of life would catch up to both Ol' Diz and his brother. Paul would win 19 games again in 1935, but then he developed a sore arm. In his remaining seven seasons, he would never again win more than five games.

Dizzy, meanwhile, put together a string of 4 straight seasons where he won more than 20 games. However, in the 1937 All-Star game, his toe was broken when it was hit by a line drive. When he tried to come back too soon from the injury, the pain forced him to change his pitching motion. That eventually ruined his arm. In his remaining three-plus seasons, he managed to win only 16 more games.

Yet even that unfortunate event eventually turned to gold for Dean. He moved almost seamlessly from the pitcher's mound to the broadcast booth, where he entertained baseball fans for the next two decades. He mangled the language, but he did it in such a humble country-boy fashion, that he permanently endeared himself to the listeners. ("If he couldn't think of the word he needed," someone once said, "he just made it up.") The charm of Dizzy Dean's life just never wore out. **TS**

# The Chance of a Lifetime

As he stepped into the batter's box, Josh Gibson knew he would never have a more important at-bat. Sure, it was just an exhibition game, but it was also the chance of a lifetime.

Gibson was the black Babe Ruth fans said, a man who supposedly once hit 75 home runs in a season. In a career that would last more than a dozen years, Gibson would win the home run crown ten times, and the batting title twice. But, of course, there was an asterisk beside those numbers. Gibson's accomplishments had come in the Negro leagues, not in the major leagues. It was difficult to tell just how good Gibson was. Oh sure, he hit more than his share of tape measure home runs, but how good was the pitching competition he faced?

That thought even nagged Gibson himself—could he really hit first-rate pitching? There was no man more anxious to prove he could play in the big leagues than Josh Gibson. Although some major league owners would talk about signing the big man, nobody would. He was not destined to be the first to cross the color line, nor even to follow the first.

This frustration must have been eating at Gibson in 1934. He was at the peak of his career, but he had to play year-round to make a living and support the two children his wife had died giving birth to. He was sure that if he was white, he would have been one of the highest paid men in professional sports, and not have to struggle to take care of his family.

Now he had his chance to prove how good he was. The great pitcher Dizzy Dean was leading a team of white major league players against a group of Negro league players in a cross-country barnstorming tour. The games were drawing great crowds, as the curious flocked to the parks to see how the great ones from the Negro leagues would fare against white players. In the first game, Gibson had been sensational, pounding

**Josh Gibson**

out three hits, including a triple, against Dean.

However, Gibson's performance had to be qualified. Critics could claim with a certain amount of truth that Dean wasn't at his best. He didn't need to be—he had nothing to prove. In fact, it could be argued that Dean took the Negro league players too lightly.

Not so here, in a game in Pennsylvania. Gibson was out to prove the previous game had not been a fluke. And after being knocked around in the first game, Dean's competitive juices were no doubt flowing, and putting a few extra miles per hour on his fast ball.

As Gibson stepped in, he knew the real test was about to begin, so he was ready. When Dean challenged him with a fastball, he smacked it high over the center field fence. And as if to show that the first one wasn't an accident, he did it again his second time up, only this time hitting it even deeper to center field. It was a moment of sweet redemption for Gibson. He had shown he could hit the best pitching the major leagues had to offer.

Ever the showman, Dean threw up his hands, walked off the mound, and into right field for the rest of the game. Afterwards, Dean congratulated Gibson. He told him that if Gibson, black pitcher Satchel Paige, and Dean were all on the same team, "We'd win the pennant by July Fourth and go fishin' the rest of the season."

Those must have been bittersweet words for Gibson to hear, for he was destined never to play an inning in the major leagues. Ironically, Gibson died of a brain tumor in January 1947, just a few months before Jackie Robinson became the first black major league player. **TS**

# Hank Greenberg's Toughest Choice

**H**ank Greenberg had a choice to make, and it was shaping up to be the toughest choice of his life.

It was late in the 1934 season, and he was playing a vital role for the Detroit Tigers, belting home runs and driving in runs for a team that had its best chance of winning its first pennant since 1907. But he was also becoming, although reluctantly, a symbol of strength for his fellow Jews.

Greenberg wasn't a particularly religious man, and he disliked the title of "the greatest Jewish slugger of all time." He wanted to be measured against every man, no matter their religion or color. However, as the season was drawing to a close, Greenberg was facing the choice of serving his religion or his game. September 10 was Rosh Hashanah, the Jewish New Year, a day to take off from work and spend

**Hank Greenberg**

in prayer. On that same day, the Tigers were scheduled to play Boston in a game many people felt was crucial to their title hopes.

Earlier in the season, Greenberg had prom-ised his parents he wouldn't play on either Rosh Hashanah or on Yom Kippur, another Jewish holiday. Now he was having second thoughts. Newspaper stories that Greenberg was agonizing over the decision stirred lively debates. One newspaper even went to one of the most well-known rabbis in Detroit to ask his opinion. The rabbi said he wouldn't have any problem with Greenberg playing on Rosh Hashanah, noting that it was a happy day that many Jews spent playing games. Yet, the dilemma still nagged at Greenberg. He just couldn't make up his mind.

Greenberg went to the park early that day. As he sat on his stool in the locker room, his teammates began wandering out for batting practice. Teammate Marv Owen asked him what the problem was. Greenberg told him he still hadn't decided what to do. Owen replied, "In 20 minutes we're all going to be out there for batting practice. The first thing that comes to your mind, do it. If it says play—play. If it says don't play—don't play."

Greenberg skipped batting practice, but when the Tigers returned to the locker room, he was still in uniform. "I'm going to play," Greenberg told Owen. And boy, did he.

In the seventh inning, he smashed a ball over the scoreboard for the Tigers first run. Then in the ninth, with the score tied 1-1, he hit another homer to win the game 2-1.

"The good Lord did not let me down," Greenberg said immediately after the game. That night, though, Greenberg heard from several of his fellow Jews. Fans and even some rabbis called him, saying he shouldn't have played. And his father called, listened to his son's reasons for playing that day, and then told him not to play in 10 days, on Yom Kippur.

Greenberg didn't. That morning he went to the synagogue to pray. When he walked in, everyone stood up and applauded.

The Tigers went on to win the pennant that season. Years later, Greenberg would write, "When I was playing I used to resent being singled out as a Jewish ballplayer, period. Lately, though, I find myself wanting to be remembered not only as a great ballplayer, but even more as a great Jewish ballplayer." **TS**

# The Great DiMaggio's Miracle Comeback

On that June morning in 1949, Joe DiMaggio opened his eyes and dreaded starting the day, much as he had every day that month and most of the days the previous month.

Each morning, his feet would touch the floor, and he'd feel the stabbing pain in his left heel. It would mean another day spent trying to answer questions he couldn't answer: "When are you going to be back, Joe? Why can't you play, Joe?" He had been out nearly two months, and there were no signs of when he'd be back. He had calcium deposits on his heels, the result of surgery to remove bone spurs. The pain would eventually stop, doctors told him, they just weren't sure when.

Meanwhile, fans were starting to mutter that the great DiMaggio was finished. And DiMaggio himself must have wondered if that,

after 10 big league seasons, two batting titles, three Most Valuable Player Awards, and his great 56-game hitting streak, this was the beginning of the end of his career.

However, on this morning something was different. As he touched his feet to the floor "nothing happened," DiMaggio said later. "I could step around the hotel room without feeling any pain. I was elated." He knew if he could walk without pain, he could very soon run, and if he could run, he could very soon play ball.

In the days that followed, he took batting practice, swinging until his hands blistered and continuing to swing until those blisters broke and his hands were bloody. When a friend expressed concern over the blood on DiMaggio's hands, he replied, "Forget about that ... There is no pain in my foot. That matters."

A few days later, DiMaggio put on his uniform and trotted out to play a game for the first time that season. It was an exhibition against the New York Giants, and although he was 0 for 4,

**Joe DiMaggio**

he was encouraged by the fact he could play the entire game. He hit a home run in a pre-game competition, and he was feeling good again. It was quite possible he'd be ready for a crucial three-game series at Boston.

When the Yankees made the weekend trip

to Boston in late June, DiMaggio went with them. He knew it wouldn't be easy. The Yankees were facing Mickey McDermott, one of the hardest throwers in the league. Initially, the kid was too fast for him. For six pitches the best DiMaggio could do was poke the ball foul to his right. Then he got a belt-high fastball that he slapped into left field for a base hit. Two batters later, DiMaggio scored. It was the beginning of one of the greatest one-man shows in baseball history.

DiMaggio hit four homers and drove in nine runs that weekend as the Yankees swept the Red Sox. He went on to hit .346 for the rest of the season, as the Yankees won the pennant over Boston by one game. And in those three days in June, the Yankee Clipper had proved to baseball fans everywhere that he was still "the Great DiMaggio." **TS**

# The Teenage Strikeout Artist

Sixteen down, one to go. Bob Feller, all of 17 years old, was having an unbelievable "summer vacation." He was going to return to high school after this adventure in major league baseball, but right now he couldn't afford to think about that.

Standing on the mound in Cleveland, looking in at the Philadelphia A's hitter, all Feller could do was to focus on the next pitch. He was just one man away from a major leagues strikeout record. To accomplish that feat he couldn't let his mind wander, couldn't think back to his days growing up on the farm, to the countless games of catch he had played with his dad on a diamond cut out of prime Iowa farmland.

The Cleveland Indians had discovered Feller while he was pitching in an amateur tournament in Dayton, Ohio in 1936. They signed him for a dollar and kept the signing secret so that Feller wouldn't lose his high school eligibility.

Then the Indians brought him along quickly, first pitching him in an exhibition against a top amateur team, and then an exhibition against the St. Louis Cardinals. Feller had been so impressive in both exhibitions, that the great Cardinal Dizzy Dean, when asked if he would pose for a photo with Feller replied, "Ask the kid if he'll pose with me." Soon after, the Indians brought him up to the big club.

At first, he was a mop up relief pitcher. Later, he was used as a spot starter, and at times he was spectacular, once striking out 15 hitters in a game. But, yes, there were also problems. Feller had a devastating fastball, but one that was hard to control. He seemed to

**Bob Feller**

have an equal chance of striking out a hitter or hitting him.

Now, on this day, he was in the ninth

inning, on the brink of a major league record. But he was also on the brink of getting the hook, at least so he thought. He had retired the first two batters, but walked the third. Leading 5-2, he still had room to make some mistakes; in his young mind, though, he thought issuing another walk or giving up a base hit would mean an automatic trip to the showers. He had already walked nine batters.

The hitter was George Puccinelli, a big man with a good batting eye. Early in a game, Feller probably would have been able to overpower him with his fastball. But by the ninth inning, Feller had lost that little something extra. Puccinelli hung in there and worked the count to 3-and-2.

Feller called time out and talked with his catcher. "We decided I might have enough gas left in the tank to throw one more good fastball," Feller later wrote. "That's what I would throw, even though it was also what Puccinelli would be expecting."

Yet, for some reason Puccinelli froze as the ball whizzed past him. It was called strike three. The game was over and Feller had his record. He returned to high school in October, the center of attention in the small town of Van Meter.

The following spring he graduated, and then returned to the Indians, where he pitched for 17 years. During his career, "Rapid Robert" won 20 or more games six times, led the league in strikeouts seven times, and finished up with 266 total victories and more than 2,500 strikeouts. **TS**

# Ted's Fantastic Finish

**T**ed Williams dug deep into his pockets as he walked the dark streets of Philadelphia on that September night in 1941, looking for a place to get the thing he sometimes craved even more than a base hit— a malt.

Williams had gone through nights like this before, times when he needed to sort through what he really felt and what he should do next. Sometimes it would comfort him to walk with one of his teammates, usually infielder Bobby Doerr, stopping for sodas along the way, talking over games and situations.

However, on this night Williams was alone—he had an important decision to make. He was in just his third season in the majors, and he was well on his way to becoming one of the greatest hitters in baseball history. He would play 19 seasons, win the batting title six times, the Triple Crown twice, and finish with a career average of .344 and 521 home runs, all this despite missing more than five seasons because of military service.

In 1941, Williams was only 23 years old, but he was having an extraordinary year. For most of the season, he had hit over .400, a great accomplishment. It had been 11 years since anyone else had hit .400, and 18 years since an American Leaguer had done it.

Going into the last day of the season, a doubleheader against Philadelphia, Williams was still hitting .400. He was actually hitting .3995, but for the record books it would be rounded up to .400. He could sit out the doubleheader, proudly point to his league leading batting average, and call it a season. It was probably the smart thing to do.

Philadelphia's Shibe Park, with it's long, late-afternoon shadows, was a tough place to hit. There was also no telling what A's manager Connie Mack would do. The A's had made it a habit of pitching around Williams. In their eight previous meetings, Williams had walked 14 times.

"It was the first time it worried me whether I was going to hit .400 or not, because the papers were writing it up," Williams said later. However, sitting out just didn't seem quite right to him. "What I was thinking was, I've been there all year, and I want to remain there. Now it's the last day and, jeez, I'm under .400."

Technically, Williams was wrong, but he didn't see it that way. "I figure a man's a .400 hitter, or he's not," he said later.

So Williams kept himself in the lineup. When he came to the plate in the first inning he was so nervous his hands were shaking. He calmed down a little when A's catcher Frankie Hayes told him that Mack had ordered them to not let up on him, but also not to pitch around him.

Williams dug in and hit a drive down the first base line for a single. It was to be the first of four straight hits, including a home run. "When I got the first hit I felt a little more confident," Williams said. "Then I hit a home run over the right-field fence and from there on, wrrooofff."

Although he was safely above .400, he would play the second game as well. He had two more hits, including another home run. His final average would be .406, and nearly 60 years later no one had yet duplicated the feat. ▪▪

# Jackie's Mad Dash Home

**A**s Jackie Robinson took his lead off third base, he must have realized he'd been there before.

It was 1955 and the Brooklyn Dodgers were facing the New York Yankees in the World Series—again. Four times since Robinson's rookie year in 1947 the Dodgers had faced the Yankees in the World Series—and four times Brooklyn had come up short. At times, Robinson had been brilliant, the 1947 Rookie of the Year, and the league's Most Valuable Player in 1949; but always he had just missed leading his team to the ultimate victory.

By 1955, at the age of 36, Robinson probably reconciled himself to perhaps never winning a World Series. However, he had done something much more significant after all, than win a championship—he had broken the color line in major league baseball. It was something that not only changed all of sports,

but also had a dramatic effect on society as a whole, helping the nation to focus on the problems of racial prejudice.

Still, Robinson and the Dodgers had come so close to a world championship several times, had endured so much just to reach this point, that losing again would be heartbreaking.

Robinson had begun his baseball career as the most aggressive, disruptive base runner since Ty Cobb. He was a royal headache to pitchers and catchers alike. He was quick enough to take big leads, resulting in easy steals or in throwing errors because catchers would have to get their throws off faster than they were used to. Not only that, but Robinson's quick, darting bluffs would distract pitchers, often causing them to walk batters.

Now, however, Robinson wasn't as big a threat as he'd once been; he had aged quickly in the majors. The stress of the verbal abuse and the prejudice he'd suffered was turning his hair gray. The aggressive base running and the cheap

Jackie Robinson steals home in the 1955 World Series

shots he endured had battered and slowed his body. He had gained weight. One reporter observed that he almost seemed portly.

Early in the regular season he fell into a slump and eventually asked to be benched. For the first time since 1949 he did not play in the All-Star game. "I'm doing as lousy as I've ever done," he said. "I can't seem to do anything right."

Then, something clicked inside him. It was as if he sensed this might be his last chance at a championship. He worked his way back into the lineup in June and batted .328 for the month.

"It's just that I made up my mind to go out there and hustle," Robinson said. "I didn't expect to have the success that I did, but I felt if I started running, the others might take the cue."

They did. For the first time, Robinson was contributing more to the club with his leadership than with his statistics. He may not have been able to hit over .300 for a season anymore or steal 35 bases, but he could help make his teammates better.

Now, in this first game of the World Series, Robinson knew what he needed to do as he led off third. He made a mad dash to steal home. It was the kind of play that would show the Yankees and his teammates that he wasn't ready to concede this Series. He just barely slid in safely under the tag. His steal had made a dramatic statement.

The Dodgers would lose that game, and the next one, but Robinson would continue to be aggressive on the base paths. Beginning with game three, the Dodgers turned things around, winning three straight. They'd lose in game six, but rebounded to take game seven and win their first world championship.

Robinson wound up batting just .182 for the Series, and his theft of home would be his only steal. He didn't even play the deciding game. Yet teammates pointed to him as one of the main reasons they finally won the World Series. **TS**

# Stan the Man's Greatest Season

In 1948 Stan Musial truly was *the Man* in St. Louis. He was in his sixth full season in the majors, and was one of the league's best players. He'd won two batting championships, two Most Valuable Player Awards, and had helped the Cardinals win world championships in 1942, 1944, and 1946.

Yet, in 1948 the Cardinals were leaning more heavily on Musial than ever before, and he was responding. Musial was in contention to win the Triple Crown—leading the league in batting average, home runs and runs batted in. And for much of the season, the Cardinals were in contention for the pennant, at least as long as Musial kept hitting. The Cardinals were lucky to win one in three games when Musial was held hitless.

That statistic moved Philadelphia manager Eddie Sawyer to say, "Of all the teams I've seen so far, Musial is the best."

Musial became more and more aware of this as the season wore down, but it didn't seem to bother him. While he was a quiet, easygoing man who shied away from the spotlight, he was also an intense competitor and a leader by example. If his team needed him to hit .400 to win the pennant, then that was what he was determined to do.

However, by September 22, the Cardinals had their backs against the wall. They were in Boston playing the first place Braves. A St. Louis loss would eliminate the Cardinals from the pennant race, and clinch the pennant for Boston. Hopes weren't very high in the St. Louis dugout as Musial stepped into the batting practice cage before the game, both his wrists heavily taped. A few days earlier, he had taken a tumble in the outfield, jamming his left wrist and bruising his right hand. It was painful for him to swing.

While his teammates were fearful, Musial

was frustrated. A sportswriter pointed out that the conditions, with the wind blowing towards the outfield, were ideal for hitters. Musial held up his wrists up in disgust and said, "Yeah, but I can't hit like this."

After some soul-searching, Musial made his decision just before game time. He tore off the tape. What followed was a clinic in intelligent hitting. With the pain, Musial couldn't afford to waste a swing—and he didn't.

In his first at-bat, he went with a pitch, stroking it into left field for a single. In his next at-bat, he patiently waited for his pitch, watching two strikes go by before he doubled. Then he homered. In his fourth at-bat he singled, and then he singled again in the eighth, to go 5-for-5. It was his fourth five-hit game of the season, tying Ty Cobb's major league record. He had done it with amazing economy, swinging the bat just five times.

More importantly to Musial, the Cardinals

**Stan Musial**

won the game, 8-2, to stay alive in the pennant race. For three days, the Cardinals would stay alive, before Boston finally clinched the pennant.

Musial wound up just narrowly missing the Triple Crown as well. In fact, he led the National League in virtually every hitting category except home runs that season. He finished second with a career-high 39, just one homer behind the co-leaders. It would be his greatest individual season. **TS**

# The Heart and Soul of the Dodgers

As Roy Campanella stepped to the plate for the Brooklyn Dodgers, he remembered the first time he had received his Dodger uniform, a little over two months before.

It was April 1, 1948—"the happiest day of my life," Campanella wrote later. "I was a big leaguer at last—with no possible chance of making the team. Yes, that was really April Fools."

It wasn't that Roy Campanella wasn't good enough to play for the Dodgers. In fact, Campanella had been told by manager Leo Durocher during spring training that he intended to make him the team's starting catcher.

Campanella was a great hitter and defensively was the ideal catcher. He was short and squat, yet he had catlike quickness and agility. He also had a great mind for the game.

Campanella was looking forward to realizing a life-long dream and playing in the majors. Sure, he knew there would be problems. As a black man, Campanella would have to endure racism and prejudice. But he figured he would have an easier time of it than Jackie Robinson, who had broken the color barrier the season before.

When Dodger general manager Branch Rickey called him into his office during spring training that season, Campanella figured it was to tell him he had made the team. Indeed, Rickey told Campanella he was the best catcher the Dodgers had, and that he was going to start the season with the big club. But then Rickey told him he'd be used as an outfielder. Campanella was stunned.

"Because I don't think you can make it as an outfielder," Rickey said. "I know you can make the Dodgers as a catcher. But I want you to help me do something bigger, something very important, to you and to all of baseball."

Rickey wanted to demote Campanella to St. Paul, Minnesota of the American Association,

thus making him that league's first black player. He wanted Campanella to fail as an outfielder with the Dodgers, so people wouldn't question Rickey's motives for sending him down. "Your failure will be a glorious success," was how Rickey put it.

Campanella was upset. He didn't want to be a pioneer; he wanted to be a player, not a pawn in a political game. Yet he also felt he had little choice. "If you want me at St. Paul, that's where I'll play. Because it's in my contract," Campanella said stoically. "For no other reason."

So by May, Campanella was in St. Paul. For a month and a half he tore up the league. Then in June, he was called back up, this time as a catcher. The Dodgers were floundering. They couldn't afford to have Campanella playing in the minors just as a political statement.

He had reported to the Dodgers just a few hours before their game with the Giants and was immediately inserted into the starting lineup. He doubled in that first at-bat. He would get three hits that night and go on a tear in which he would get 9 hits in his next 12 at-bats.

From that time on, no one could think of an excuse to send him back to the minors. For ten seasons, Roy Campanella would be the heart and soul of the great Dodger teams of the 1950s. He was the league's Most Valuable Player three times—in 1951, 1953, and 1955. His great defensive ability and deft handling of the pitching staff helped the team win five pennants and a world championship.

Tragically, Campanella's great career was cut short in 1958 when he was left permanently paralyzed following an auto accident. Although his playing days were over, Campanella battled back, remaining part of the Dodger organization, and serving as a source of inspiration for people everywhere. **TS**

# A Pitching Marathon to Remember

It was a little bit hard for the San Francisco Giants to fathom. Here was a 42-year old pitcher shutting them out through 9 innings, through 10 innings, through 11, through 12. . . .

Warren Spahn was, in the words of *Los Angeles Times* sportswriter Jim Murray, "at an age where he's almost too old to run for president, and when a good runner can beat his fastball to the plate." Yet, on July 1, 1963, age didn't seem to matter. The Giants just couldn't score on Spahn. However, Spahn's team, the Milwaukee Braves, couldn't score on Giants' pitcher Juan Marichal either. So on they went into the night, through 13 innings, 14 innings, 15. . . .

Spahn's baseball career had gotten off to a late start. After coming up to the majors briefly in 1942, he served the next three years in the military and was wounded in combat. He didn't get his first major league win until 1946, when he was 25 years old.

Spahn proved to be a late bloomer, though. In his 21-year career, he'd win 20 or more games 13 times, finishing with 363 total victories, the most by any left-hander in history. At the age of 39 he threw his first no-hitter; he threw his second five days after his 40th birthday. As he lost speed on his fastball he came to rely more and more on his screwball and his experience. He became an expert in keeping batters off- balance with his varied pitch selection.

"He doesn't frighten you," the Dodgers Maury Wills once said. "He's not a guy you don't want to hit against. In fact, you can't wait to hit against him. But, when you get there, you're like a guy going backwards in a revolving door."

Spahn liked to say, "Hitting is timing. Pitching is upsetting timing."

Now, on this breezy night at Candlestick Park, Spahn had the Giants upset. They were hitting his pitches—Spahn would only strike out two—but either someone was always there to field it, or the wind knocked it down. In the ninth inning, it looked as if Willie McCovey had put an end to it when he drove a ball into the right field stands. But the first base umpire ruled it a foul ball.

Giants' manager Alvin Dark reportedly asked his pitcher Marichal if he needed to come out; Marichal, 16 years Spahn's junior, said he could last just as long as Spahn could.

"I said to myself three times, 'This will be my last inning' " Marichal said. "Each time I went out there again."

In the 14th inning, the Giants looked on the brink of breaking through, with runners on first and second with none out. But Spahn wriggled out of that jam, getting the final out with the bases loaded.

In that inning, Spahn had intentionally walked Willie Mays to set up a possible double play. It was the first walk Spahn had given up in 31 2/3 innings.

In the 16th inning, Spahn faced Mays again. This time he tried to start him with a strike. "I threw Mays a screwball that hung," Spahn said. "It didn't do a thing."

Mays smashed it over the left field fence to end the 16-inning marathon after 4 hours and 10 minutes.

Incredibly, both pitchers had gone the distance; Marichal had thrown 227 pitches, Spahn 201. Managers in this day and age would never allow their pitchers to throw that long, but it didn't seem to hurt either player. That season Marichal would win a league high 25 games. Spahn would win 23. Spahn retired two years later, ironically, finishing his career with the Giants. **TS**

# The Harmonica that Helped Win a Pennant

As Yogi Berra sat near the front of the bus, he could feel the long fuse to his temper burning to an end.

For years he had been the good time guy, the guy who was always in favor of a good laugh, even if it was at his expense. His refusal to take himself and situations too seriously had helped him become one of the all-time great catchers.

Now, however, as manager of the 1964 New York Yankees, he was finding that his easy-going nature was working against him. When Berra was offered the job at the start of the season he jumped at the chance, but, at the same time, he knew there would be problems.

Mickey Mantle and Whitey Ford, the leaders on this veteran team, were also Berra's long-time pals, pals who loved to make fun of the short, roundish catcher. They had respected Berra as a player, but didn't exactly stand back in awe when he spoke.

When a reporter asked Mantle what he thought of the hiring, Mantle said, tongue-in-cheek, "I think we can win in spite of it."

Berra had spent a long time working on his opening speech to the team. He was going to tell them with mock seriousness that there were going to be strict new rules about behavior and off-field activities. Then, after an appropriate pause he would break into a grin and tell them he was just kidding, that the important thing was they all play hard and have fun. It would be just the right mix of authority and humor ... or so he thought. As Berra started to wrap up the first part of the speech, Mantle loudly announced he was quitting, inferring that the new rules would drive him to it. Berra's punchline was ruined.

To make matters worse, the Yankees

**Yogi Berra**

weren't as talented as in years past. Oh sure, they still had the big names, but those veterans were wearing down. The team couldn't just show up and expect an automatic win anymore. They weren't young or hungry. There were times when Berra felt they just didn't care.

This August evening was one of those times. The Yankees were stuck in third place. They had just been swept by the White Sox in a four-game series and now were stuck in traffic on the way to the airport. It was hot, and Berra was fuming at how miserably his team had played. Suddenly, he heard someone playing a harmonica in the rear of the bus.

Berra yelled to knock it off. Phil Linz, a back-up infielder, put down the harmonica for a moment and then asked Mantle what Berra had said. With a straight face, Mantle said that Berra had said to "play it louder." Linz tried his best to comply. Understandably, that brought Berra out of his seat and back down the aisle until he stood over Linz and screamed at him.

Obviously stunned, Linz tossed the harmonica to Berra, who in turn slapped it away. It hit Joe Pepitone in the knee, and he hammed it up, crying "Oh, my knee, my knee!"

It didn't seem like it at the time, but it was a turning point for the Yankees. It seemed to snap them out of the doldrums and put Berra in a different light. No longer was he just a clown.

The Yankees put together a spectacular September to win the pennant. The World Series with St. Louis went seven games, but the Yankees wound up on the short end.

In many people's eyes, Berra had proven himself as a manager, a guy who could motivate a team when necessary. Unfortunately for him, the Yankees didn't agree. They fired him after the season and hired the St. Louis manager to replace him.

It was a humiliating moment, but one that didn't finish Berra. He would go on to manage again, during the 1970s with the Mets and once more with the Yankees during the 1980s. **TS**

# The Chairman
# of the Board

On Whitey Ford's shoulders sat the burden of the 1960 World Series. No, he hadn't cost the Yankees the world championship that year. And he hadn't cost long-time manager Casey Stengel his job after that painful seven game Series loss to the Pittsburgh Pirates.

However, for Ford, the unspoken leader of the Yankees, the responsibility of making his teammates forget about the previous season was there when he received the nod to start the first game of the 1961 World Series.

Although this was a team that would be best remembered for the slugging of Mickey Mantle and Roger Maris—who broke Babe Ruth's single-season home run mark that year with 61—the real key to the 1961 World Series against the Cincinnati Reds was pitching.

There had been no better pitcher in 1961 than Ford. New manager Ralph Houk had asked Ford to pitch every fourth day, rather than every fifth day as Stengel used him. Ford had flourished; not only did he tie a career high for appearances with 39, he won a league high 25 games, the first 20-game winning season in his ten year career.

More than that, he had been a steadying influence in the locker room. Coaches thanked him publicly for being open to doing things differently than in the past. They knew very well the weight Ford carried in the clubhouse. He was called the Chairman of the Board.

Off the field, Ford loved to have a good time, and he and Mickey Mantle could party up a storm. On the field, Ford was all business. He got along well with his teammates, particularly since he didn't publicly criticize them or show them up. If they made an error in the field, you never saw him react in anger or dismay.

"When Whitey pitched, we knew we'd win the first game of any series," Yankees' third baseman Clete Boyer said. "Whitey was a great pitcher, but it was more than that. Having him on the mound gave us such a feeling of confidence. He'd pitch, we'd win, and that was how it was."

Here in the 1961 World Series, the Yankees needed just that. There were just too many other things that could hurt their confidence. Mantle was out of the opener because of an injured hip. Maris was about to go into a hitting slump.

If Ford felt any pressure, though, he didn't show it. He was a cool customer on the mound, not overpowering, just consistent in throwing tough pitches. The Reds pounded ground ball after ground ball at Boyer at third base. And Boyer was magnificently efficient, making both the spectacular plays, throwing runners out from his knees, and all the routine ones.

Ford gave up just two hits and one walk in a complete game victory. The Reds never got a runner past first base. They never hit a ball to the warning track. The Yankees had captured the all-important opener, 2-0.

In the fourth game, Ford virtually locked up the Series, shutting out the Reds for five innings before having to leave after twice banging foul balls off his toe. The Yankees won 7-0 to take a three games to one lead. They closed out the Series in the next game.

With his 14 scoreless innings added to his previous World Series appearances, Ford broke Babe Ruth's World Series record of 29 and 2/3 consecutive scoreless innings pitched. Ford was named the Series MVP.

"Poor Babe," Ford joked afterwards. "It's been a tough year for him." But it was a great year for Whitey Ford. **TS**

# The Duke Breaks Out

**D**uke Snider stood alone in the Dodgers' dugout, looking pale and upset. It was August of 1952, and Snider, the man who had once been called "the jewel of the organization," the man with "the perfect swing," had just been benched indefinitely. The Dodgers were unhappy with Snider's effort and his emotional outbursts. He was mired in a slump, hitting .280. The team could tolerate his average, but not his temper tantrums. After striking out, which he did fairly often, he was known to throw bats and destroy water coolers. The Dodgers had thought he would grow out of this behavior. After all, he had already been in the major leagues for three full seasons.

Instead, he was getting worse. His moodiness was reflected in his play. There were times he didn't run out ground balls, times he didn't go all out chasing fly balls. So the Dodgers benched him.

Duke Snider

"My problem was that I had excelled in athletics all my life and that I really didn't know what adversity was until I came to the Dodgers," Snider said years later. "I had to learn that every day wasn't a bed of roses, and that took some time."

So deep down, Snider understood and accepted his benching. What he didn't like was the way it was reported in the newspapers. One New York writer had called him a crybaby. Another had written that the Dodgers were looking to cut his salary and unload him.

The worst thing, though, was he hadn't read this for himself. The benching and the articles about it happened at the start of a road trip. Snider was in Cincinnati when his wife called, crying, and read him the news.

Now, before the Cincinnati game Snider demanded to know who told the writers that his salary was going to be cut. Dodgers' manager Charlie Dressen just shrugged his shoulders and said he didn't remember telling the writer any-

thing. Snider would later have suspicions.

"Dressen knew how to handle me," Snider said. "He'd get me mad, and then I'd go out and take it out on the opposing club. Sometimes I needed a fire lit under me."

So, for three days Snider sulked. And on the fourth day, he was a new man. He started hitting and didn't stop. He hit over .400 in the last month of the season. In the 5-4 win over Philadelphia that clinched the pennant in late September, Snider drove in the winning run with a double.

"How was that perfect swing?" he yelled out at the writers.

Snider stayed on a tear through the World Series, hitting four home runs and driving in eight runs, although the Dodgers lost in seven games to the Yankees. The next season, he doubled his regular-season home run production, hitting 42, the first of 5 straight seasons in which he hit 40 or more home runs. In 1955, he again hit four homers in the World

Series, this time leading the Dodgers to their first world championship.

Snider played for the Dodgers for 16 seasons; he was an excellent outfielder and a fine hitter. During the 1950s, his name always came up when New York baseball fans argued as to who was the best center fielder in baseball—the Giants' Willie Mays, the Yankees' Mickey Mantle or Snider. The fact that he was often mentioned with the great Mays and Mantle is evidence of what kind of ballplayer the "Duke of Flatbush" was. **TS**

# The Man Called "Mr. Cub"

For two straight seasons, Ernie Banks had been the best player in major league baseball—playing for one of the worst teams, the Chicago Cubs. To the amazement of many, he had done so with a big smile on his face.

By 1961, however, many people were wondering just how long Banks could keep up that cheerful demeanor. There were chinks showing in his armor. A knee injury limited his range at shortstop. His batting average had fallen from above .300 to around .270. He was 30 years old, and time was beginning to catch up to him. Perhaps it was time for a change.

Banks had been the Cubs' starting shortstop since 1954. In 1958 he was voted the National League's Most Valuable Player as he hit .313 and led the league with 47 homers and 129 RBIs. He won the award again in 1959, hitting 45 homers and leading the league in RBIs with 143.

"During my first 26 years in baseball, Joe DiMaggio is the only player I'd ever consider rating ahead of Ernie Banks after the year Ernie had for me in 1959,"said Bob Scheffing, Banks' former manager. "He batted fourth behind three hitters who didn't even average .260, and still he batted in 143 runs. I figured out that his bat was directly responsible for 27 of our 74 victories that season. In the field he was the equal of any shortstop I've seen."

In 1961 the Cubs traded for an infielder who played shortstop, and were faced with the problem of what to do with Banks. Finally, in May of that season they moved him to left field.

"Only a duck out of water could have shared my loneliness in left field," Banks wrote later. "I had never played the outfield and the first thing I thought about was all the tricky wind currents."

He may have been uncomfortable there, but he didn't complain. For 23 games he played solidly, if unspectacularly at the position, getting as much help and advice from his teammates as possible.

The Cubs were aware of Banks' discomfort and appreciative of the effort. In mid-June, Elvin Tappe, the Cubs head coach asked Banks about switching to first base. Banks jumped at the chance.

That night he borrowed a glove, got a few last second pointers, and took the position. Although he would make some fundamental errors initially—including taking a throw with two feet directly on the bag, begging for an ugly collision—he was good enough so that everyone realized he had perhaps found a new home there.

That season Banks alternated between first and shortstop, and the following year he moved to first permanently. He'd play 10 more years there, continuing to put up great offensive numbers; he finished his career with 512 home runs and 1,636 RBIs. Although he never got a chance to play in the post season, his undying enthusiasm for the game became legendary throughout baseball, justly earning him the nickname, "Mr. Cub." **TS**

## The Mick Blasts Past the Babe

As he began to walk toward home plate, Mickey Mantle paused a moment and turned back to his teammate, Elston Howard.

"Elston," Mantle said. "You might as well go back to the clubhouse, because I'm going to hit the first pitch out of here for a home run."

The score was tied 1-1 and it was the bottom of the ninth in the third  game of the 1964 World Series. In season's past, Howard might have done just that, or believed he could have. The Yankees, led by Mantle, had been nearly invincible, going to six of the past seven World Series. But this season, everyone knew they had been lucky just to make it to the Series.

Mantle had missed nearly half the 1963 season with a broken foot, and when he returned he wasn't the same dominating presence he'd always been. Mantle and the Yankees were

**Mickey Mantle**

aging, and that year the Dodgers swept them in four games in the Series. In 1964, under new manager Yogi Berra, the Yanks floundered through much of the season. Mantle was still hitting the ball, but he was struggling in the outfield. The team looked undisciplined, making costly, silly mistakes. By September, many people were writing them off.

Then things all started to come together. Mantle moved over to right field, where there was less pressure on him defensively. And the Yankees picked up two pitchers—Mel Stottlemyre and Pedro Ramos—who were unbeatable down the stretch. The team put together an 11-game winning streak and rallied to win the pennant. Now, they were locked in a heated battle with the St. Louis Cardinals for the world championship. The Series was tied at one game apiece.

Mantle had not exactly covered himself with glory so far. In the fifth inning, his error in right field had put a Cardinal runner in position to score the tying run. As he waited for the ninth inning to start, though, Mantle saw his chance at redemption. Barney Schultz had taken the mound, relieving starter Curt Simmons.

Schultz was a right-handed knuckleball pitcher and had been the team's top reliever all season, with 14 saves and a 1.65 ERA. But for Mantle, Schultz was a dream come true.

Mantle loved to hit knuckleball pitchers, especially from the left side. His swing from that side (he was a switch hitter) was long and looping, sometimes not quick enough to get around on hard throwers. However, it was perfect for slow knuckleballs, especially ones that don't move and dance as they're supposed to when they approach the plate.

Mantle knew from scouting reports that Schultz had a tendency to throw just that type of pitch early in the count to get a strike. As he turned away from Howard and back toward the plate, his mouth was watering.

Schultz's first pitch was just what Mantle

was looking for. He took a vicious swing and sent it soaring into the third deck in right field, as 67,000 fans roared their approval.

Not only had Mantle won the game, he had broken Babe Ruth's record for most career home runs in the World Series. That record meant a lot to Mantle. As the heir to the great Yankee legends of the past—Ruth, Lou Gehrig, and Joe DiMaggio—Mantle had a strong desire to see his name alongside theirs in World Series glory.

Mantle would go on to hit two more home runs in the Series, but the Yankees would lose the championship, four games to three. Mantle would play four more years, but 1964, when he hit .303, had 35 homers, and drove in 113 runs, was his last truly good season. His retirement closed out a golden era for the Yankees. During his 18-year career, they had won 12 pennants and 7 world championship, and Mantle had been the biggest reason for their success. **TS**

# The Greatest Catch of All Time

To a man, the Cleveland Indians knew just what Willie Mays could do. Even though Mays played in the National League for the New York Giants and the Indians were in the American League, for years they were the only two teams to hold spring training in Arizona. Each spring, the Indians had watched Mays seemingly play the entire outfield by himself, catching balls that no one else could even hope to reach.

When the two teams met in the 1954 World Series, though, the Indians were more concerned about Mays' bat. He had been the N.L. batting leader, hitting .345 with 41 homers, and 110 RBIs. If they could contain Mays at the plate, the Indians felt their outstanding pitchers could take care of the rest of the Giants. So did most of the country. The Indians—winners of an American League record 111 games during the

**Willie Mays**

season—were heavy favorites.

Game one boiled down to a pitching battle, with the Giants' Sal Maglie matching Bob Lemon, a 23-game winner that season. It was 2-2 in the eighth when Maglie began to crack. First he walked Larry Doby. Then Al Rosen reached on an infield single. There were none out and slugger Vic Wertz was coming up. Wertz had owned Maglie, hitting a triple and two singles in his previous three at bats. Giants' manager Leo Durocher looked to the bullpen and brought in left-hander Don Liddle.

In addition to all his great natural talent, Mays had the ability to think through situations, to position himself where he could make great plays. This time was no exception. "Wertz had been getting around well all day, and in this situation, two runners on, I figured he'd be likely to try to hit behind them so they could advance," Mays said later.

Mays also knew that many hitters like to swing at a new reliever's first pitch, so he was on his toes. Liddle threw a fastball and Wertz smacked it hard. "It went off Vic's bat like a cannon shot," said Rosen.

It was a line drive that rose as it headed toward the outfield. In center field, Mays turned and starting sprinting toward the outfield wall. His hat flew off.

"I had this sinking feeling," said Rosen, who had a perfect view of the play as he ran toward second base. "I could tell that if the ball stayed in the park, Willie would catch it."

It did stay in the park. About 460 feet from home plate, in full sprint, Mays stretched out his arms and made the over-the-shoulder catch. And then he did something almost as remarkable. Knowing that there were no outs, he spun

around and fired the ball to second base, hoping to keep the runners from tagging up and advancing. Doby did manage to tag up and reach third, but was held there by Mays' throw. Rosen was frozen at first, as 50,000 fans cheered wildly.

After Mays' catch, Liddle was taken out; when he handed the ball to the relief pitcher he said (with a smile on his face), "Well, I got my man."

The Indians appeared to be broken. They stranded Doby and Rosen and lost the game in extra innings. The Giants would go on to sweep the Series in four straight.

Mays' great catch became a signature play in his 22-year career, one filled with hundreds of brilliant defensive plays, as well as tremendous offensive accomplishments—3,283 hits, 660 home runs, and 1,903 RBIs. Twice voted the league's Most Valuable Player, many fans who witnessed Mays' exploits on the diamond called the Say Hey Kid the greatest all-around player in history. **TS**

# Crowning a New Home Run Champion

As Hank Aaron stepped to the plate for the Atlanta Braves in their 1974 home opener, he took a deep breath. He had come such a long way for this opportunity. And it had been a journey that just seemed to get tougher the closer he got to his goal.

Aaron had come up to the Milwaukee Braves in 1954, seven years after Jackie Robinson had broken baseball's color barrier. Yet Aaron still had to endure racial prejudice, at times being forced to stay in separate hotels and eat at separate restaurants from his teammates because he was black. Now, 20 years later, as he drew within range of breaking Babe Ruth's career home run record, he had endured more bigotry, including hateful mail and even death threats.

Yet, through it all his teammates marveled at how he seemed to remain unshaken. Even when baseball commissioner Bowie Kuhn ruled that Aaron would have to play in the Braves' opening series in Cincinnati, possibly denying him the chance to tie or break the record at home, Aaron seemed more bemused than anything else.

"It was the first and last time I can ever think of that a player was actually thrown into a game," Aaron would write later. He had hit the tying homer in the Braves' first game, and then he had to deny charges that he was purposely trying to avoid hitting the record-breaker when he struck out twice and grounded out in the second game of the series.

That had all led to this moment against the visiting Los Angeles Dodgers. It had been declared Hank Aaron night, and the Braves drew the biggest crowd in their history. Only Kuhn was a no-show; he was at a speaking engagement in Cleveland, and this offended Aaron. Some predicted that all those distractions and pressures would keep him from hitting the record-breaker that night. But the pressure, said Aaron, just helped him focus even more. All he wanted to do, he said later, was just get it over with.

Dodgers' pitcher Al Downing walked Aaron his first time up, and started him off with a ball in the dirt the next time. The Dodgers were leading 3-1 at the time, and there were two outs with a runner on first. Downing did not want to walk Aaron and bring the go-ahead run to the plate.

His next pitch was a slider, low and down the middle. Aaron smacked it. The ball kept rising until it reached the outfield, then it cleared

**Hank Aaron hits his record-breaking 715th homer**

the wall and went into the bullpen, where Braves' reliever Tommy House snagged it.

As the crowd stood and cheered, Aaron trotted slowly around the bases. House ran in from the bullpen to give Aaron the ball.

Aaron was greeted at home plate by a swarm of his teammates, photographers, and his mother. A great sense of pride and relief showed on his face. The quiet, skinny kid from Mobile, Alabama—the player many pitchers called the best pure hitter in baseball—had broken a record once considered unbreakable, and he'd done it with the dignity and class that defined his entire career. **TS**

# Clemente Comes Through in the Clutch

J udging from his stats, the Pittsburgh Pirates couldn't ask much more of Roberto Clemente.

After all, the veteran outfielder was batting over .500, as well as making some outstanding plays in the field. However, the Pirates needed something more to overcome the Baltimore Orioles in the 1971 World Series. It was game three of the best of seven Series, and the Pirates were down, two games to none. Only four other teams had ever rebounded from such a deficit. Compounding the difficulties, the Orioles were hot, having won 16 straight games. To turn it around, heck, just to be competitive, the Pirates needed something intangible, a wake up call, a shot in the arm. . . in short, all the things critics had said Clemente couldn't give a team.

Of course, this had always been the rap on Roberto Clemente. He would give you good numbers—hits, runs, runs batted in—and he'd play solid defense, throwing runners out with his tremendous arm. But he wouldn't play every day. He'd whine about mysterious injuries and then pout if someone questioned their validity. He would complain about field conditions, what kind of dirt was under home plate, how many potholes were in the outfield. More times than not, it sounded as if he was making excuses.

The Pirates and their fans had noticed somewhat of a change beginning in 1966. That season Clemente played in 154 games, had career highs in home runs and RBIs, and was the league's most valuable player. Still the Pirates only finished in third place. Now here in 1971, on baseball's biggest stage, Clemente finally had the chance to prove he was a clutch player and team leader.

The Pirates were nursing a 2-1 lead when Clemente came up to start the bottom of the seventh. He badly wanted to plant one in the outfield seats to give the Pirates an insurance run. As a result, he probably swung a little too hard at a pitch by Mike Cuellar, topping it and sending it dribbling back to the mound.

Although it appeared to be a routine out, Clemente ran hard out of the box. When Cuellar looked up, preparing to make the throw, he was shocked to see Clemente closing so fast on the bag. Cuellar suddenly realized he had no time to dally, so he rushed the throw. It was a bad one, pulling the first baseman off the bag. Clemente was safe.

Cuellar was visibly shaken. He walked Willie Stargell on four straight pitches. That brought up Bob Robertson, who missed a bunt sign, but then homered to put the Pirates up 5-1, the eventual winning margin. In the box score, Clemente's play didn't look that significant, but in the Pirates' clubhouse it was huge. It signaled a turnaround for the team. "You watch Roberto and you can't help getting all psyched," said Pirate outfielder Gene Clines. "There's the old man out there busting his butt on every play of every game. Look, I'm 25. If he can play like that, shouldn't I?"

The Pirates did, taking three of the next four games to win the Series. Clemente continued on his hitting tear, batting .414 with two homers and two doubles. And he continued to play great defense in right field. Not surprisingly, he was voted the Series MVP.

"I want everyone in the world to know that this is the way I play all of the time," he said after the Series. Everyone did.

Tragically, Clemente played only one more season. On New Year's Eve 1972, he was killed in a plane crash while taking relief supplies to earthquake victims in Central America. **TS**

# The Sweetest Championship

Years before, Al Kaline had made a promise to himself—he would not attend a World Series game until he played in one. And after leading the American League in hitting in his second year, it seemed as if he might not have to wait too long. That was 1955. However, over the next 13 years, Kaline's team, the Detroit Tigers, had not won a pennant, finishing as high as second only twice in that time. Now, though, in 1968 Detroit had finally made it to the Series, and were facing the defending world champs, the St. Louis Cardinals.

It should have been sweet for Kaline, especially after he had been forced to miss much of the season because of a broken arm. But it wasn't. There were whispers that Kaline, now 36, belonged on the bench, that he was just in the starting lineup for sentimental reasons and that his presence would hurt the team. Those were the kind of whispers that bothered a proud man like Kaline.

Indeed, the Tigers had made moves to insure Kaline a starting spot in the Series. During the regular season, Kaline had returned from his injury and couldn't budge his replacement, Jim Northrup, out of right field. So instead, he platooned with Norm Cash at first base for the rest of the year.

For the Series, though, the Tigers benched their starting shortstop, moved their center fielder there, slid Northrup into center, and put Kaline in his usual spot in right. It was a gutsy move, but it didn't pay off at first. Kaline hadn't exactly set the world on fire in game one. He had doubled, but he had also struck out three times in a 4-0 loss.

In game two, it looked as if the Cardinals might jump off to an early lead as they put runners on first and second with one out. Orlando Cepeda then hit a long, foul ball to right that

**Al Kaline**

seemed headed for the seats. But Kaline gave chase, snagging the ball just before he stumbled through an open gate. He then spun around and fired the ball into third base to hold the runners.

The next batter also hit a ball to right field and Kaline made a difficult catch look easy to end the inning. Those plays turned the momentum. Kaline got two hits and scored two runs as the Tigers won 8-1. The Series was tied one game apiece.

"Now we go back to Detroit, and after all these years without a World Series, it should be something to see," Kaline said.

It was, but that didn't seem to bother the Cardinals. They won the next two games, taking a three games to one lead. Then in game five, also in Detroit, the Cardinals, with a chance to close out the Series, took an early 3-0 lead. The Tigers chipped their way back until they trailed 3-2 in the seventh. With one out and the bases loaded, Kaline stepped up to bat. The crowd was on its feet.

"When I saw all those people standing I got goose bumps," Kaline said later. He stroked a single to center field, driving in the tying and go-ahead runs. Detroit held on for a 5-3 victory.

In the next game, Kaline went 3 for 4, and drove in four runs to lead a 13-1 Tiger rout. Detroit then beat Cardinal ace Bob Gibson in game seven to win its first World Championship since 1945.

Kaline hit .379 for the Series with two home runs and eight RBIs. It turned out to be his only trip to the World Series, but he'd certainly made the most of it. ■TS■

# A Grueling World Series Win

**S**t. Louis Cardinals pitcher Bob Gibson couldn't remember being as weary as he was today, taking the mound for the seventh game of the 1964 World Series.

Just two days before he had pitched ten innings to win game five. He had also pitched seven innings in game two. And he had pitched four innings of relief in the last game of the regular season. Two days before that he had pitched eight innings. He had a right to be tired.

"I wasn't sure I didn't belong on the shelf, having pitched four grueling games in ten days, Gibson wrote later. "But I couldn't beg off with my manager and teammates depending on me."

One thing Gibson did have going for him was adrenaline. He was so pumped up to be pitching the deciding game of the World Series against the New York Yankees, that he didn't feel the pain and stiffness in his arm at first. In the first two innings, he struck out three batters. After three shutout innings, though, the adrenaline began to wane. He noticed he wasn't getting the same speed on his fastballs, and it was getting tougher and tougher to hit the spots he wanted.

Luckily for Gibson, the Cardinals had jumped out to a 6-0 lead by the fifth inning. In the sixth, the Yankees began to get to him. With two men on, Gibson faced Mickey Mantle, who earlier in the Series had broken Babe Ruth's record for World Series career home runs. Gibson had been having great success beating Mantle with fastballs on the outside corner of the plate. This time, however, he couldn't get it past him. Mantle homered to make it 6-3.

Cardinals' manager Johnny Keane went to the mound, looked into Gibson's eyes, and asked him how he felt.

"Naturally, I lied," Gibson said. Keane might have known he was lying, but he stayed with his veteran. Gibson got out of the inning. He was hit hard in the seventh and eighth, but the

Yankees couldn't break through. He went into the ninth leading 7-3. In the dugout before he went back to the mound, Keane gave him some quiet words: "Just throw fastballs; the Yankees can't hit four homers in an inning."

Gibson struck out the first batter, but the next batter homered, making it 7-4. Gibson was getting nervous, but he remembered Keane's words. He reached back and struck out pinch-hitter Johnny Blanchard. Then he tried to throw a fastball past Phil Linz. Linz planted it in the left field bleachers. Now it was 7-5, and the next batter was Bobby Richardson, who already had 13 hits in the Series.

In the bullpen, Ray Sadecki was warming up. A trip to the showers for Gibson seemed imminent as Keane headed toward the mound. But the manager didn't make the move, deciding to stick with Gibson through at least one more batter.

When Keane was later asked why he didn't make the obvious move he said, "I had a commitment to his heart."

Gibson didn't let him down. He came inside with a fastball to Richardson, who popped it up for the final out. Gibson had his second Series victory, and the Cardinals had a World Championship. During the remainder of the decade, Gibson would shine in two more fall classics—1967 and 1968—and finish his career with a brilliant 7-2 record, 1.89 ERA and 92 strikeouts in World Series competition. **TS**

## Two Days Rest and a Blazing Fastball

**A**bout the third inning, Sandy Koufax realized his curveball wasn't going to work this day.

It was game seven of the 1965 World Series against Minnesota and Koufax was pitching on just two days rest. He knew he was just going to have to gut this one out, and try to win on the strength of his will and his blazing fastball.

Koufax had done that before. In fact, in his first six seasons in the major leagues he had done little else. He had used his overpowering, but sometimes erratic, fastball to win games. However, he was very inconsistent, sometimes unable to throw strikes when he needed to. Entering the 1961 season, he was not even a career .500 pitcher.

Then in a spring training game before that season against, ironically enough, Minnesota, Koufax discovered he was a better pitcher if he didn't only rely on overpowering hitters. He had been scheduled to throw just five innings. However, the pitcher who was supposed to pitch the last four innings never showed up. Since the Dodgers were short of pitchers, Koufax had to pitch longer.

Dodger catcher Norm Sherry suggested that Koufax ease up on his fastball and throw more curves in order to conserve his strength. Koufax complied and was pleasantly surprised. Not only was he able to keep the batters off-balance with his curveball, he had new found control of his fastball. He threw seven no-hit innings.

"I came home a different pitcher from the one who had left," Koufax said. In the next six seasons, Koufax became the most dominant pitcher in baseball, winning 129 games while losing only 47, pitching four no-hitters, and capturing three Cy Young Awards.

In the 1965 Series' deciding game, he was again facing the Twins, but his curveball wasn't working. That would be a problem for most pitch-

**Koufax smiles for photographers after pitching his fourth no-hitter**

ers against a Minnesota team that had some notoriously good fastball hitters. But not for Koufax. He reached back and overpowered the Twins.

In the first eight innings, Koufax hit just one rough spot. In the fifth inning, the Twins had runners on first and second with just one out. Koufax escaped the jam when Dodgers third baseman Jim Gilliam made a diving stop of a ground ball and scrambled up to get a force out at third. Then Joe Nossek grounded out to end the inning.

In the ninth, Koufax had just one thing in mind:

"I'm not going to walk a man if I can possibly help it." First, he got Tony Oliva to ground out. Then Harmon Killebrew singled to left, bringing the tying run to the plate.

Koufax bore down and struck out Earl Battey on three straight pitches. Next came Bob Allison, who worked the count to 2 and 1. One after another, Koufax threw fastballs on the outside corner. Allison went for both and missed both. Koufax had the win, and the Dodgers had their world championship.

In 1966, Koufax may have had his greatest season. He won 27 games, had an ERA of 1.73, and led the Dodgers to another pennant. Although they were swept in the Series by Baltimore, at only 30, Koufax seemed to have his best days ahead of him.

Instead, Koufax shocked the baseball world by retiring, citing the excruciating pain in his pitching elbow. He felt that the days he could win just on the strength of his will and his fastball were over. **TS**

## An "Old Man" of 30 Gets Revenge

The words echoed through Frank Robinson's mind most of the season— "Robinson is not a young 30 years of age."

Every time he stepped to the plate during this 1966 season, he thought of those words. Every time he let loose on the base paths, he thought of them. Every time he needed to make a defensive play. . . .

Now, standing in the outfield at Yankee Stadium, he was probably thinking about that as his Baltimore Orioles tried to hold on to a 7-5 lead against the Yanks. He was anxious to prove he was just as vital, talented, and enthusiastic as he had ever been.

For ten years, Frank Robinson had been the shining star of the Cincinnati Reds. In 1961, he had been the National League's Most Valuable Player, and had led the Reds to the pennant. In 1965, he was still at the top of his game, hitting

.296, with 33 home runs and 113 runs batted in.

Following that season, however, he was traded to Baltimore for Dick Simpson, a light-hitting outfielder, Milt Pappas, a slightly above average starting pitcher perhaps on the downside of his career, and Jack Baldschun, a mediocre relief pitcher. When asked why they would make such an apparently one-sided trade, Reds general manager Bill DeWitt implied that Robinson's best years were behind him. He said although Robinson was only 30, his body had taken a lot of abuse. "Robinson is not a young 30 years of age," DeWitt said.

There was some truth to that. Robinson had taken more punishment than an average 30-year old player. In six of his ten seasons in the National League he was hit by more pitches than anyone else. He also had a reputation for running into outfield fences and having nasty collisions at the plate. Quite bluntly, he seemed to give up his body every game to make a play. In addition, DeWitt implied that Robinson—a serious and somewhat sullen ballplayer—was not the most positive influence in the Reds' clubhouse.

However, Robinson felt he still had plenty of good years left, and he was determined to prove that DeWitt had made a mistake. Besides continuing to play with unmatched intensity and aggression, Robinson also made a conscious effort to be more of a leader in the clubhouse.

"I took a new approach," Robinson said. "I wasn't going to stop knocking the shortstop on his butt when sliding into second. But I made an effort to be more outgoing, to be more relaxed, and to smile more."

That made the transition to Baltimore a little smoother. What really did the trick, though, was his performance on the field. And it wasn't just the numbers—he would win the Triple Crown that season—but his hustle and self-sacrifice. Nowhere was this more evident than in that game at Yankee Stadium. The Orioles led 7-5 in the bottom of the ninth, but the Yankees had two men on. Roy White then hit a line drive that seemed destined to land in the bleachers.

Robinson sprinted to the wall, then leaped high against it, stretching over the top and toppling into the crowd. When umpire Hank Soar came over, Robinson had the ball in his glove, having robbed White of the winning home run. It was the type of play a man who was an "old 30" would never make.

That season the Orioles went on to win the World Series, and Robinson won the league's MVP Award, becoming the first player to win it in both leagues. It was sweet revenge, and it quieted that voice that kept saying he was an old 30. **TS**

## The Incredible Scoreless Streak

**D**on Drysdale had just walked the bases loaded in the bottom of the ninth inning. In his mind, he kept repeating his credo—one pitch at a time, one batter at a time. His team, the Los Angeles Dodgers, was leading 3-0, so he could afford to make a small mistake and still win the game. However, there was more at stake than just this one game.

Coming into that night in late May 1968, Drysdale had pitched 36 consecutive shutout innings. It was a stunning achievement, more so because it had been accomplished by a pitcher on the downhill side of his career.

Drysdale was in his 13th season of what turned out to be a 14-year career. Sure, he was still tough to score against; his 2.74 ERA the previous season was proof of that. Still, he had been only 13-16 in each of the previous two years, after averaging more than 20 wins a season

Don Drysdale breaks the record for consecutive scoreless innings pitched from 1962-1965. Perhaps all that was on his mind this night as he stared in from the pitcher's mound at Dodger Stadium toward the hitter, Giants' catcher Dick Dietz.

The count was 2 and 2; the next pitch was a slider that came in and hit Dietz in the elbow, and he headed to first base. Then all hell broke loose.

"After he took one step toward first base, he was called back so quickly (by the umpire) that there wasn't much doubt in my mind what was happening," Drysdale said later.

The umpire had ruled that Dietz hadn't made an honest effort to avoid being hit, and thus was not entitled to first base. The Giants, led by their manager Herman Franks, went crazy. They protested long and loud, the game was delayed nearly half-an-hour, and Franks was ejected.

When the game finally resumed, Dietz fouled off the first pitch and then hit a shallow fly to left field. It wasn't deep enough to allow the runner on third to tag up and score. There was one out.

Pinch-hitter Ty Cline was next. Cline hit a scorcher to first base. Wes Parker fielded it and threw to the plate for the force out. Two outs. Finally, it was up to Jack Hiatt, another pinch-hitter. He popped up to first base.

The Giants' threat was over, and so was the game, and Drysdale's amazing streak was intact.

"Dodger Stadium went wacko," Drysdale said. "There were 46,067 fans there that night, and they made enough noise for twice that many people."

In Drysdale's next start, against Pittsburgh, he threw another shutout, his sixth straight, breaking a major league record. Only one more record stood in Drysdale's path: Walter Johnson's record of 56 consecutive scoreless innings.

Drysdale broke that in his next start, against Philadelphia. However, that game also marked the end of his streak. In the fifth inning, the Phillies' Tony Taylor scored on a sacrifice fly.

The streak ended at 58 2/3 innings.

"I think my first reaction was one of relief that it was over," Drysdale said. "I knew it couldn't go on forever, and it had gone on a whole lot longer than I expected."

The crowd at Dodger Stadium gave Drysdale a standing ovation. The next batter stepped in and tipped his cap to the pitcher. "I nodded back," Drysdale said, "and went back to work." **TS**

# The Dominating Dominican

**S**an Francisco Giants' manager Herman Franks stood in his office, scratching his head as reporters peppered him with questions. "How bad is Marichal's injury? How long will Marichal be out?"

Franks had no answer for them. He had long ago quit trying to figure out Juan Marichal, the Giants' star pitcher. Franks just knew that his Dominican ace would ultimately come through.

"I don't know, why don't you go ask him," Franks said.

It was 1966, and the Giants were in the midst of a tight pennant race. Yet, little things were starting to go wrong, especially with Marichal. His pitching hand had been slammed in a car door, his back was bothering him, and now his left ankle hurt after he had twisted it.

He had complained of being in pain, and even asked to miss a start because of the nagging injuries. Still, it was hard to determine just how hurt he was. Marichal had a 17-5 record already, and was one of the most dominating pitchers in the majors. He had won 20 or more games three straight seasons, and would eventually wind up with 243 career victories. Franks probably wished all his pitchers could be so banged up.

The Giants' skipper had learned that you could get great things out of Marichal with a little push, but if you pushed too hard, he could snap. Last season Marichal had lost his temper and become involved in a brawl with Los Angeles Dodgers' catcher Johnny Roseboro. Fans and players alike were horrified as Marichal hit Roseboro in the head with a bat, resulting in a two-week suspension for the Giants' ace.

Marichal had tried to put that incident in the past, but the memory dogged him. He felt that no one really understood his side of the brawl, that he was just trying to defend himself.

With all that working on his psyche, Marichal pushed himself out onto the mound to start against Cincinnati in a late August game. He still had problems with his ankle and couldn't push off hard enough to get extra juice on his fastball. But he figured he had already missed one start, it was time to get back.

He wasn't spectacular, but he was solid against the Reds, until the fourth inning. That's when Tommy Helms drilled a line drive right back up the mound. The ball nailed Marichal in the right foot.

Franks was beside himself as he came to the mound, muttering, "first the left foot, now the right." Marichal, himself in a bit of shock, said later the first thing that came to his mind was, "At least it will cure my limp."

He didn't leave the game, though. Despite the pain in his feet, he pressed on, eventually winning 6-3. The win put the Giants in first place. After the game, Marichal had his right foot X-rayed. The doctor looked at the X-ray and shook his head.

"Did I break my foot?" Marichal asked.

The doctor shook his head again, and said that yes, there was a break, but not from what happened against the Reds.

"I know," Marichal said. "It happened four years ago, at Los Angeles." The doctor was amazed. "You won 90 games since then on a broken foot?"

The doctor determined that Marichal's old injury had healed, and now he seemed healthy enough to keep pitching. And pitch he did— he went on to win 25 games that season, including three crucial games down the stretch; still, as often happened during the mid-1960s, the Giants fell just short of winning the pennant, finishing a game behind the Dodgers. **TS**

## Brooks Brings the Orioles All the Way to the Top

It had been tough for Brooks Robinson and his Baltimore Orioles teammates to forget about 1969. The Orioles had been so good in the regular season, and then fallen flat on their faces in the World Series, losing in five games to the New York Mets.

Now, as they took the field against the Cincinnati Reds in the 1970 Series, Robinson couldn't help but think of his miseries the previous October. It had been a lackluster season for him in which he batted a career-low .234. But he seemed to recover by the American League Championship Series, batting .500. The World Series, though, had been a disaster. Robinson was befuddled by Mets' pitching, and went 1 for 19 at the plate. Some had said it was a sign that, at age 32, he was past his prime.

Robinson didn't agree, and he soon proved it. In 1970, he batted .276 and drove in 94 runs dur-

**Brooks Robinson**

ing the regular season; then he hit .583 in the Championship Series as the Orioles once again swept the Minnesota Twins. He was itching to have a great World Series.

However, once the Series began, it wasn't Robinson's bat that made people stand up and notice—it was his glove work. In the sixth inning of the first game, he amazed spectators when he made a diving stop of a sharp grounder by Lee May behind third base, whirled off-balance, and fired a perfect one-hopper off the turf to first for the out. It was to be just the first of several spectacular defen-

sive plays by Robinson.

Robinson's next big contribution was to come with his bat. With the score tied at 3-3 in the seventh inning, he golfed a pitch over the left field fence for a home run that gave the Orioles the win.

Robinson picked up the fielding heroics again in game three. With the Series tied at a game apiece, the Reds looked ready to get off quickly as they put their first two runners on base. Then Tony Perez made the mistake of hitting a grounder in Robinson's direction. He gobbled it up to start a double play. Next Robinson made a leaping catch of Johnny Bench's low line drive to end the inning. In the bottom of the first, the Orioles scored two quick runs on Robinson's bases-loaded double, and went on to win 9-3. Cincinnati won game four, but the Orioles closed out the Series in five games the next day.

Of course no one who had followed Robinson's career up until then should have been surprised at his brilliant defensive work. For years he had been considered the best fielding third baseman in all of baseball.

Still, his teammates good-naturedly poked fun at the way Robinson seemed to take over the Series with his glove. Teammate Frank Robinson fined him in kangaroo court for "showboating" during the Series. For good measure, while he was dazzling people with his glove, Robinson was also hitting. He batted .429, drove in a team-high six runs, and was voted the Series MVP.

"I hope we can come back and play the Orioles next year," Bench said after the Series. "I also hope Brooks Robinson has retired by then." **TS**

## The Day Yaz Brought Home a Pennant

You couldn't see it from the grandstands at Fenway Park, where fans were screaming their lungs out, but as Carl Yastrzemski stepped to the plate in the final regular season game of 1967, there was a battle going on inside him.

He was in the spot he always dreamed of. The Red Sox trailed 2-0, but the bases were loaded and there were none out. If the Red Sox lost, their season would be over. If they won, they would either be in a special playoff series, or the World Series.

It was a spot where a hero would hit a homer to break the game open. A voice inside Yastrzemski's head—along with a lot of voices in the stadium— said to swing for the fences. But another voice echoed inside the head of the man they called Yaz. It was softer, more reasonable.

Yaz had been bigger than life that season. He

led the league in hitting, runs batted in, and was tied for the lead for homers. It was in the last two weeks of the season, though, when Yaz had been just awesome. He had hit over .500, driven in 16 runs, scored another 14, and hit 5 home runs as the Sox won 8 out of 12 games. He had virtually carried the Sox, keeping them in the pennant race, although many had picked them to finish near the bottom of the league.

Going into this last game of the regular season, the Sox were tied for first with their opponent that day, the Minnesota Twins. Detroit, which was playing a doubleheader, was just half a game behind.

With that in mind, Yaz had every right to swing for the fences when he came to bat in the sixth. He was smarting a little bit after committing an error that allowed the Twins to score one of their runs.

However, as he walked to the plate, he battled with his emotions. On the mound was Dean Chance, a pitcher who threw a mean slider.

Most times when a hitter tried to pull that pitch and drive it into the stands, it would go straight at the shortstop and result in a double play. Yaz knew that would kill the Sox momentum and probably their pennant hopes.

"As I put dirt on my hands, I started a litany," he said later. "Base hit, base hit, base hit. Up the middle. Don't try to pull the ball."

Yaz did hit it up the middle, singling in the tying runs. The Twins came undone after that, as the Sox scored three more times for a 5-2 lead. In the eighth, Yaz ended a Twins comeback by pegging a base runner out at second with a tremendous throw from the base of the outfield wall. The Sox held on in the ninth for the win and at least a tie for the pennant. When Detroit split its doubleheader later that day, Boston had its pennant and a trip to the World Series.

"I've never seen a perfect player, but you were one for us," Boston manager Dick Williams told Yaz later. "I never saw a player have a season like that." **TS**

# The Inspired Comeback

For Willie Stargell, the time for inspirational speeches and quiet words of wisdom was over. It was time to put up or shut up.

It was the seventh inning of game seven of the 1979 World Series. The Pittsburgh Pirates were trailing the Baltimore Orioles 1-0. There was a runner on first base and Stargell was at the plate. He knew he might not get another chance to be a hero.

The 38-year old Stargell had been the Pirates emotional and spiritual leader. He had preached the virtues of teamwork to his teammates, talked about self-sacrifice and contributing to the whole. He took to giving out stars to teammates for their outstanding performances in areas not always mentioned in the press or revealed in the box scores.

His work in the clubhouse had done wonders, helping bring together one of the league's most culturally and temperamentally diverse teams. It had helped them rally in September to edge the Montreal Expos for the National League Eastern Division title. And it had helped the Pirates rally from a three games to one deficit in this World Series.

Stargell never discounted how important leadership skills were, once stating, "People don't realize that there are a lot of emotions in baseball, or how much pride and deep feelings are worth."

Now, however, the Pirates needed more than just his leadership. They needed his bat. Stargell had faded in September that season, batting just .222 for the month. However, he knew his job wasn't to get on base, it was to knock guys in, usually with home runs. He had done just that, hitting four game-winning homers that month, finishing the season with 32.

Stargell had been even better in the playoffs, hitting two homers and batting .455 in a sweep of the Cincinnati Reds in the National League

Championship Series. But Stargell knew all that would be for naught if he failed here. When Pittsburgh had fallen behind 3-1 in the Series, many wondered out loud if the Pirates would quit. They didn't, of course, and Stargell's leadership was a major reason why.

Now, as he stepped to the plate, he summoned up not inspirational words, but all of his 17 years of major league experience. He was batting against left-hander Scott McGregor. That season, Stargell had problems pulling the ball against left-handers; he just wasn't quick enough anymore to get around on them. On this day, however, he borrowed a lighter bat from a teammate. He was sacrificing a little power to get a better cut at the pitch.

McGregor started him out with two fastballs, high and tight. This meant just one thing to Stargell: the

**Willie Stargell**

next pitch was going to be a breaking ball. Stargell told himself to be patient, the key to hitting a breaking ball was to delay your swing just a bit. Stargell waited, and then swung the bat like a war club and connected. The ball flew into the right-field bleachers. Stargell had hit his third Series homer; the Pirates went on to win the game and the Series.

Stargell was voted the Series MVP. He told a national television audience that he would love to cut the trophy up and give a little bit to each one of his Pittsburgh Pirates family.

"A lot of guys say things like that," one teammate said later, "but this guy means it."

# The Sweet Vindication

**A**s he always had, Joe Morgan of the Cincinnati Reds wanted this chance to be the hero—or the goat.

He was standing in the on-deck circle in the ninth inning of the seventh game of the 1975 World Series. The Reds and the Boston Red Sox were tied 3-3; there were two outs and a runner on third. And Morgan expected Boston to walk Pete Rose to get to him. After all, it had happened before. The Red Sox had left-hander Jim Burton on the mound and Rose was a switch hitter. The percentage play would be to walk Rose and pitch to Morgan, a left-handed hitter.

However, the Red Sox were not eager to face the 5-foot-7 Morgan. They knew that since he had come over from the Houston Astros in 1972, he had become the linchpin for this talented Reds squad. From 1973 to 1977, he had averaged 22 home runs and 60 stolen bases a season. In 1975, Morgan hit .327, drove in 94 runs, and would be named the league's Most Valuable Player. Morgan said later that there were seasons when he had better numbers, but he never had a better year.

So with the game—and the Series—on the line, the Red Sox chose to pitch to Rose, who had batted .317 that season and driven in 74 runs. "When I saw (Red Sox catcher Carlton) Fisk get down in his crouch, I couldn't believe it. I yelled at him, 'Hey, what's going on!'" Morgan recalled later.

Morgan badly wanted to win this Series. When he came over from the Astros, his new manager, Sparky Anderson, said he was the final piece to the Reds championship puzzle. Yet, the team nicknamed the Big Red Machine still had no championship. In 1972, the Reds had reached the World Series, but had been beaten by the Oakland A's. The next season, the Reds had been upset by the New York Mets in the National League Championship Series. Morgan didn't want to go down in the history books as the key player on an overrated team.

As Morgan watched from the on-deck circle, the Red Sox went after Rose; but they didn't give him anything good to hit. He worked a walk out of it. "I was the happiest guy in the place," Morgan said.

This at-bat would be no cake walk though. While Burton, was only a rookie, he was throwing with the poise of a veteran. He threw a hard slider, which was a difficult pitch to drive. The count went to 2 and 2. Burton threw the slider and Morgan, just trying to protect the plate, hit it. It wasn't much, a blooper of a fly ball, but it was enough to do the job. The ball fell in for a base hit, scoring the run that put the Reds ahead for good and gave them the world championship. Although it wasn't spectacular, it was sweet vindication for Joe Morgan. **TS**

**Tom Seaver**

# The Mainstay of the Miracle Mets

Tom Seaver was pumped up. He was just three outs away from winning his first World Series game and giving his team, the New York Mets, a three games to one lead in the best of seven series. All he had to do was shut out the Baltimore Orioles in the ninth inning, much as he had the previous eight. But, it wasn't going to be as easy as it looked.

Seaver had been the mainstay of the 1969 Miracle Mets. He had a 25-7 record that season with an ERA of 2.21. He had been overpowering, and after spending only two seasons in the majors, he had led the Mets—for years the laughingstock of the league—to the division title.

However, in the playoffs he had been much less dominant. While he had beaten the Atlanta Braves in game one, they had hit him pretty hard, scoring five runs on eight hits. Then Seaver had lost the World Series opener to Baltimore, giving up four runs in only six innings. So, going into game four, Seaver clearly seemed vulnerable.

In this game, though, Seaver was pitching much as he did during most of the regular season. At times he was overpowering, but mostly he was smart, and after eight innings, he was ahead 1–0. It was a tenuous lead, but Seaver felt it would be enough as he headed out to the mound for the ninth inning.

The first batter flied out. Then Frank Robinson singled, which brought up Boog Powell, the Orioles leading home run hitter. Seaver pitched him carefully, but he also singled, moving Robinson, the tying run, to third. Mets' manager Gil Hodges came to the mound, ready to call to the bullpen. Then he asked Seaver how he felt. "A little tired, but nothing serious," Seaver answered.

Hodges hesitated, then left the mound. He was going to give Seaver a chance to climb out of the hole he was in. Truthfully, it might not have been the best decision. Seaver had lost his best stuff, and he was going to need some luck to get by. He got some, though not as much as he hoped.

Brooks Robinson hit a line drive to right field that looked as if it was going to fall, but Ron Swoboda made a spectacular diving catch. Had it gotten past him, the Orioles would have scored two runs. As it was, they were held to one when Frank Robinson tagged up and just beat the throw home. Elrod Hendricks then hit a long drive that twisted foul at the last minute. On a full-count, he flied out to right field. Seaver had escaped, but just barely.

When the Mets couldn't score in the bottom of the ninth, Seaver went out to the mound for the tenth inning, making sure not to make eye contact with Hodges. Seaver wasn't sure he could finish this game, but he wasn't going to ask out.

In the tenth, Baltimore's leadoff hitter reached on an error. The next batter popped out, but the batter after that, Clay Dalrymple, singled, putting runners on first and second with one out. Mets' pitching coach Rube Walker came to the mound to talk to Seaver.

"I'm tired, Rube, but I don't think I'm at the end of my rope," Seaver said. "I've got a few pitches left." Walker nodded and went back to the dugout.

The next batter flew out to right field, advancing a runner to third. The next batter was Paul Blair, one of the Orioles best hitters. Somehow, Seaver reached down and threw two fastballs past Blair. He then struck him out on a breaking ball. He was exhausted, but he had gotten out of the inning.

"Let's get a run," Seaver yelled to his teammates before they came up in the bottom of the tenth. The Mets did score; they won 2-1, and went on to win the Series the next day. It was a perfect ending to a miracle season. **TS**

# Palmer's Last Stand

It was kind of strange for Jim Palmer, going to the mound for the deciding game of the Baltimore Orioles season.

Oh, it wasn't strange to be out there in an important game. Jim Palmer had been there quite often in his 17-year career. It was just strange to be out there after the way this 1982 season had begun.

Jim Palmer was 36-years old. For years, he'd been one of the most dominating pitchers in the American League, winning 20 games or more eight times, and winning three Cy Young Awards. But in 1981, he had finished 7-8 and it appeared as if time—and more than 3,000 innings pitched—was beginning to take its toll on him.

In 1982, several sportswriters suggested that Palmer be demoted to the bullpen. The Orioles front office demanded he be taken out of the starting rotation. Finally, after some delibera-tion, manager Earl Weaver called Palmer into his office.

For what seemed like forever, Weaver had been a thorn in Palmer's side. They had first met in Palmer's second year. Palmer was temporarily on his way down the chain with a sore arm, Weaver was working his way up as a gifted man-ager. Palmer expected a Yoda-like figure who would immediately cure his arm problems. What he got was a grumpy little guy who told Palmer how to pitch—and it wasn't long before Palmer came to feel Weaver didn't know what he was talking about.

"I learned a lot from Earl Weaver," Palmer wrote later. "The first thing I learned was that he didn't know a thing about pitching."

However, Weaver did know how to handle players, and how to light a fire under Palmer. By the time Palmer had worked through his arm troubles and gotten back into the big leagues, Weaver was the Orioles' manager. Together they helped Baltimore dominate the American

League, winning four pennants and a world championship in 1970.

In 1982, Weaver was in his last season as manager and he was determined to do things his way. He talked to his coaches and they told him Palmer still had enough to start. "I'm sending you to the bullpen," Weaver told him. "But I still think you can win a lot of games."

Palmer wasn't a relief pitcher for long. After about a month, he was given the chance to start and wound up pitching eight shutout innings in a win against Oakland. It was the 250th victory of his career, and he hardly seemed ready to stop.

Palmer won 11 straight after that, as the Orioles chased down the front-running Milwaukee Brewers. Going into the final weekend of the season, Milwaukee was four games up on the Orioles, with four games to play—all at Baltimore.

The Orioles won the first three, leaving Weaver with one of the most important decisions of his career: who to start in the deciding game. He didn't hesitate, he picked Palmer.

"At the time, I might not have admitted it, but I guess I was as nervous before that game as I was before the (World) Series in 1966, or 1970," Palmer said later. "I really wanted it, for the come-from-behind aspect of it, and for the team, and for. . .OK, I had a lump in my throat for the maniac I'd been playing under for all those years."

Unfortunately for Palmer, Weaver, and the Orioles, it didn't work out quite the way they hoped. Baltimore lost the game 10-2, and the division title with it. But Weaver would never say he regretted the decision to start Palmer. The aging pitcher had finished with a 15-5 record, and put the Orioles on the brink of a great comeback. He had just fallen a little short. **TS**

# Rollie Rings Up
# the Reds

Oakland A's pitcher Rollie Fingers could sense Dick Williams coming out of the dugout and heading toward the mound even before he saw him.

It was the ninth inning of the seventh game of the 1972 World Series, and Fingers thought it was over for him. The A's were clinging to a 3-2 lead over the Cincinnati Reds when Fingers hit pinch-hitter Darrel Chaney with a pitch. That brought up Pete Rose, who, with two outs, represented the winning run.

Fingers had been brilliant this Series, in fact, all season. He was redefining the role of a relief pitcher. He was becoming a "closer," the pitcher saved for the last few outs of a game, years before there was such a thing. He had worked in 65 games that season, winning 11 and saving another 21.

His handlebar mustache had also come to symbolize the free-spirited A's, a group of highly talented, young players who had a hard time following strict rules, but who still managed to put together win after win. Most of them had mustaches, some had beards, and almost all of them had long hair.

This World Series against Cincinnati, whose players were required to have short hair and be clean shaven, had been dubbed the Hairs against the Squares.

Fingers had worked in six of the seven games, and in three of the five American League Championship Series games before that. He was tiring now. The Series had been a nailbiter, as five of the previous six games had been decided by just one run. Cincinnati had been the favorite to take the Series, especially with A's slugger Reggie Jackson out with an injury.

Now, it had come down to the last half inning, and Fingers was faltering for one of the few times that season. He'd already worked out of one jam in the eighth inning, when the Reds had the tying and go-ahead runners poised on second and third with two outs. Fingers had gotten Denis Menke to fly out to end that threat.

In the ninth, though, Fingers didn't think he was going to get an opportunity to work out of another jam. Williams was making his way to the mound. Fingers knew what Williams wanted to do. Rose was a switch-hitter who batted left-handed against the right-handed Fingers. Rose had batted better from that side of the plate, and Williams had left-hander Vida Blue in the bullpen ready to come in and turn Rose around.

On the way to the mound, A's catcher Dave Duncan intercepted Williams. "I know what you're going to do," Duncan told his manager. "Don't do it. Rollie is throwing as good as I've ever seen. He can get Rose."

Williams listened to Duncan. He hadn't gotten to where he was by just managing by the numbers; but sticking with Fingers was going to require a leap of faith. He took the leap.

Rose jumped on Fingers' first pitch and hit it to left field. But outfielder Joe Rudi was there to make a routine catch. Oakland had won the world championship.

It would be a springboard for both Fingers and the A's. They won the next two World Series, with Fingers winning Series MVP honors in 1974. By the time he retired in 1985, Fingers had accumulated 341 saves—more than any other reliever—and in 1981, received both the American League's Cy Young Award, and its Most Valuable Player Award. **TS**

## The Day Catfish Proved His Point

Jim Catfish Hunter was not a happy camper. As was his usual practice, he showed up early for this game in 1968 to take batting practice before pitching against the visiting Minnesota Twins. Although Hunter made his living as a pitcher for the Oakland A's, he prided himself on his hitting. This time, though, when he tried to take his turn in the batting cage, manager Bob Kennedy dismissed him. "Get outta there. Let some real hitters hit."

Kennedy's remark was somewhat in jest. Hunter didn't take it that way, though. He was upset, and this perceived snub brought all his frustrations into focus. For three seasons he had pitched well, at times very well. He had pitched three shutout innings in the 1966 All-Star

Catfish Hunter

game, and he had a 2.81 ERA in 1967. Eventually, he would become a first-rate, big-time pitcher—five straight seasons with 20 or more victories, and 9 more wins in post-season play. However, at this point in his young career, Hunter had yet to have a winning season. He was too inconsistent, and frankly his team wasn't very good; the A's had finished last twice in the past three seasons.

Now, as he went out to the mound to start the game, Hunter was determined to direct his anger into his pitching. He was so focused, that it wasn't until the seventh inning that he realized he had a no-hitter going, in fact, a perfect game.

In the stands and in the dugout, though, it was a different story. Hunter's wife was sitting among the other player's wives, wringing her hands, and wiping tears from her cheeks. Hunter's teammates were avoiding him in the dugout, not wanting to ruin any good luck he had going. In the outfield, rookie Joe Rudi was just hoping he wouldn't screw up a play.

On the mound, Hunter made up his mind just to go for it. No more curves or change-ups—he was going to throw only fastballs and sliders. For eight more outs, Hunter remained perfect.

Finally, with two out in the ninth he faced pinch-hitter Rich Reese. Reese was only in his second full season in the majors, but the year before he had proved to be an exceptional clutch hitter. He had been 8 for 13 in pinch-hitting appearances the previous September.

Reese fouled the first ball off, then took two balls. On the fourth pitch he took a swing, and missed. Hunter thought he had the strikeout on his next pitch, but the umpire called it a ball, making it a full count. Hunter knew he had a no-hitter going, but he didn't realize he hadn't walked anyone. One more ball was going to ruin the perfect game.

Reese, meanwhile, wasn't going to budge. He was going to swing at everything close, determined not to look at a third strike. Hunter threw a fastball. Reese fouled it off. Hunter threw another fastball. Reese fouled it off. And on it went, for five straight pitches. Finally, on the sixth straight fastball, Reese swung and missed. Hunter had pitched the first perfect game in the American League since 1922.

In the A's locker room afterward it was almost as if they had won a World Series—everyone was excited and the champagne flowed. After calling home to North Carolina, Hunter stuck his head into Kennedy's office. Lost in the perfect game celebration was the fact Hunter had three hits and three RBIs in the 4-0 win.

"Well, Mr. Kennedy," Hunter said. "Can I hit now?"

Kennedy just smiled and said, "Kid, you can do anything you want." **TS**

## Three Mighty Swings

Reggie Jackson had noticed something a little different in batting practice. He had that special feeling. Just before game six of the 1977 World Series against the Los Angeles Dodgers, he seemed to have more pop in his bat, more sweetness in his swing. And he could see the ball, perhaps better than he'd ever seen it. "It looked like a volleyball," he said later.

However, Jackson wasn't going to get overly hyped up. He had been excited before, only to wind up disappointed. This entire season with the Yankees, in fact, had been one long emotional roller coaster. He had been welcomed with open arms—and an open checkbook—by owner George Steinbrenner, only to be shunned by his manager, Billy Martin. He had alienated his teammates by saying in a national magazine interview that he was "the straw that stirs the drink," among the Yankees, and virtually insulting team captain Thurman Munson at the same time.

**Reggie Jackson**

Jackson had won his teammates back late in the season, though, when he was moved to the clean-up spot in the order and helped carry them to a division title. Then, in the deciding game of the American League Championship Series he had been benched, only to come up with a crucial pinch-hit that helped the Yankees make it to the World Series.

So, a good, almost magical, batting practice meant nothing to him. That season, he felt like things could change in a heartbeat, and they often did. The Yankees were leading the Series three games to two, and were back in the friendly confines of Yankee Stadium for game six. Jackson was already having a terrific Series, with six hits in 17 at-bats and two home runs. Even so, nothing hinted at the performance he was about to give.

In his first at bat, Dodgers' pitcher Burt Hooten walked him on four straight pitches. In the fourth inning on the first pitch, Jackson got the end of his bat on the ball and drove it into the right-field bleachers. When Jackson came up again in the fifth inning, this time he faced relief pitcher Elias Sosa. He was shocked when Sosa threw him a fastball down the middle. Jackson drove this one into the right-field bleachers as well. Going back to game five, when he had homered in his last at-bat, the last three times Jackson had swung the bat he had homered.

Jackson realized he was on a terrific tear, and prayed for the chance to bat again before things changed. That chance came in the bottom of the eighth inning. The pitcher was Charlie Hough, a guy who relied on a knuckleball, a pitch that was either impossible to hit or impossible to miss, depending how the air took it.

Jackson reveled in the moment, as the crowd chanted "Reg-gie, Reg-gie." "Hough threw me a knuckler," Jackson recalled. "It didn't knuckle."

Jackson crushed the ball, sending it nearly 500 feet to dead center field into a sea of empty black seats. The crowd roared as Jackson stepped out of the dugout for a curtain call. He'd hit three homers—on three successive pitches—and tied Babe Ruth as the only player to hit three homers in one Series game. The Yankees won the game that night, and the Series; and the roller coaster season of 1977 had finally ended—with Reggie Jackson on top.     **TS**

## A Dismal Season Ends in Triumph

As Johnny Bench came to the plate in the ninth inning of game four of the 1976 World Series, he focused himself. His Cincinnati Reds were grinding their way to a second straight world championship, but Bench wanted to go for the kill now. He was determined not to let even one game get away. This one-sided World Series against the New York Yankees must have been such a bore to many fans, Bench thought; but to him, it was wonderful, and the sooner they got it over, the more wonderful it would be.

The ending to the previous season had been so nerve-racking for Bench and the Reds, as Cincinnati beat the Boston Red Sox in one of the most competitive and memorable World Series in history. That had been followed by one of Bench's worst ever regular seasons. He had been plagued by cramps and back spasms most of the season, and hit just .234.

The cramps and spasms "affected my swing, my throw to second, my entire game," Bench said later. "I tried everything to correct the problem, but nothing worked."

There were whispers that Bench was washed up, that now was the time to trade him. Bench just kept plugging away, though, and the Reds kept winning. Late in the season, he changed his diet to include more salt. That, in turn, seemed to relieve much of the cramping. Once that happened, his hitting started coming around.

The Reds swept Philadelphia in the National League Championship Series to advance to the World Series against the Yankees. For Bench, it was like a breath of fresh air. Relatively pain free, baseball was fun again for him, and he was playing like it.

The Reds had a three games to none lead against the Yanks, and Bench was streaking. Earlier in game four, he had stroked a two-run homer to left field to give the Reds a 3-1 lead.

However, the Yankees had refused to go quietly into the night. Entering the ninth, the Reds were clinging to a 3-2 lead.

As he waited his turn to bat, Bench realized the importance of the inning. The Yankees Thurman Munson was due up fourth in the bottom of the ninth, and he had been unstoppable. The Yankees' catcher was batting .529 for the Series, and already had four hits that day. Bench felt a one-run lead wasn't going to be enough.

Bench stepped to the plate with two men on and one out. He was thinking about just making contact to drive in an insurance run. But when a fat pitch came down the middle he couldn't resist—he crushed it for a three- run homer that broke the Yankees back.

The Reds went on to win the game 7-2, giving them a four-game sweep. Bench hit .533, with two homers and six RBIs, and was named Series MVP. For him, the win was even sweeter than 1975. "To do it again in 1976, with the dismal season I had—that was a personal triumph." **TS**

# One Memorable World Series Moment

I f there really was going to be a storybook ending to this game—the sixth game of the 1975 World Series—then it was appropriate that Carlton Fisk would be the one to write it.

The game had been an emotional roller coaster ride for Boston Red Sox fans. The Red Sox were on the brink of elimination, trailing in the best of seven series three games to two, to the Cincinnati Reds, a team many people felt was the best in baseball.

The Sox had fallen behind 6-3 in the eighth inning. It was enough to make even the staunchest New Englander pack his bag and mutter about the curse—the one that held that the Red Sox would never win another world championship after they traded Babe Ruth to the Yankees in 1920.

However, the Sox received a second life when pinch-hitter Bernie Carbo hit a three-run homer in the eighth inning. In the ninth, the Sox loaded the bases with none out, but couldn't get the winning run across.

So, the two teams battled into the 11th inning. With one man on and one out, Reds' second baseman Joe Morgan hit a drive that looked like it was going out. But at the last moment, right fielder Dwight Evans made a leaping catch at the wall. He then fired the ball back to the cutoff man who threw to first for a double play.

In the 12th, the Reds threatened again, but this time stranded two runners. By the time Fisk stepped up to the plate in the bottom of the 12th, it was 12:33 a.m. and everyone was exhausted.

It had started out to be such a dismal season for Fisk. He had suffered a broken forearm in spring training when he was hit by a pitch. That had cost him more than half the season. When he came back, however, he was nearly unstoppable. In 79 games, he hit .331 and had 52 RBIs.

In the American League Championship Series, when the Red Sox swept the three-time defending champion Oakland A's, Fisk hit .417. But what endeared Fisk to Boston fans most was that he was one of their own, not only New England born and raised, but New England tough through and through. So fans could be sure that if Fisk was exhausted, he wasn't going to let it affect him.

On the second pitch he saw, Fisk hit a high, deep drive to left field. There was no question it was going to clear the fence. The question was whether it was going to stay fair. Fisk stopped a few feet up the line toward first base and anxiously watched, waving the ball with both arms, *willing* it to stay fair. All of Boston, perhaps all of the nation, held its breath and watched. Finally, it hit the foul pole screen for a game-winning home run.

Fisk leaped with joy, thrusting his two fists into the air. He virtually danced around the bases as the Fenway Park fans went crazy.

The Red Sox lost game seven and the World Series the next night, making Fisk's homer bittersweet. However, the dramatic ending of game six—and the lasting television replay image of Carlton Fisk "waving" the ball fair and jubilantly running around the bases—stands out as one of the most memorable moments in baseball history.　**TS**

# Ryan's Record-Breaking Night

As he was leaving home for the ball park, Nolan Ryan heard his wife calling him back.

"Don't take any chances out there," she said. "You have your whole career ahead of you, and the strikeout record isn't worth risking your arm. You'll have other chances."

Ryan reassured his wife. He'd play it safe; if he didn't get enough strikeouts that day to break Sandy Koufax's single-season record, he'd try to pitch again on Sunday, his team's last game of the season.

It was 1973, and Ryan was finishing up a career-best season with the California Angels. He had come over from the New York Mets the season before, vowing to make his former team regret the trade. They did. Ryan won 21 games in 1973, and threw two no-hitters. He was only 26 years old; he would go on to pitch another 21

Nolan Ryan sets a new single-season strikeout record

seasons, throwing an incredible 5 aditional no-hitters, and striking out a record 5, 714 batters.

Now, going into his final start of the 1973 season against the visiting Minnesota Twins, Ryan was 16 strikeouts short of breaking Sandy Koufax's record of 382 for a season.

It was a strange atmosphere in Anaheim that night. A great play by an Angels' infielder would bring boos, a great catch by an outfielder would get jeers. The fans were there to see a strikeout record. In the first inning, it looked as if they might see Ryan leave for an early shower, as Minnesota scored three runs. But the Angels scored three runs of their own in the first, and Ryan settled down.

Ryan struck out 12 through five innings, and then struck out the side in the seventh to pull within one strikeout of the record. In the eighth, he struck out Steve Brye, tying the record.

In the ninth, however, he began to tire. Oh, he still held the Twins scoreless—he hadn't given up a run since the first inning—but he didn't strike anyone out and that made things even stranger inside the park. With the score tied in the bottom of the ninth, the fans were rooting for the Angels not to score. They wanted the game to go into extra innings, giving Ryan another chance at the record. It did. In fact, it went through a scoreless tenth, and when a weary Ryan came back into the dugout after that, manager Bobby Winkles looked into his eyes. Winkles must have been thinking the same thing Ryan's wife had told the pitcher earlier: it just wasn't worth the risk.

"The eleventh is going to be your last inning," Winkles told him, "No matter what, you can't go on."

So Ryan went out to the mound for the eleventh knowing that if he was going to break the record, it would have to be now.

Brye was the first batter up, and Ryan got two strikes on him. He fouled off the next pitch and then popped out.

Ryan walked Rod Carew and then got Tony Oliva out on a fly ball (the crowd booed). Ryan would have just one more chance, but even that was almost taken away from him. Twice Rich Reese swung and missed, but on the second pitch, Carew tried to steal second. Angels catcher Jeff Torborg reacted out of instinct and came up throwing. The throw was perfect, and for a moment it looked as if Ryan's bid for a record would end on the base paths.

It was a close play, but Carew was called safe. The crowd cheered, "and then (they) started to boo me," Torborg said later.

Given life once again, Ryan threw the ball as hard as he could. Reese took a big cut and missed. The crowd stood and roared. Ryan had the record.  **TS**

## The Day Schmidt Went Wild at Wrigley

I t wasn't the way Mike Schmidt had hoped to start the season. After two banner years in Philadelphia when he'd led the league in homers, Schmidt had hoped to start 1976 with a bang. Instead, the first week had been a fizzle. He had just 3 hits in his first 18 at bats, and had struck out 9 times.

Now, as the Phillies came in to Wrigley Field to face the Chicago Cubs, Schmidt had been dropped from third to sixth in the lineup. It was shaping up to be a perfectly miserable afternoon.

Schmidt knew though that he couldn't let himself get too down about it, just the way he couldn't let himself get too pumped up when things were breaking his way. He had discovered early in his career that the key to success was keeping an even emotional keel. He'd started to become a dominant power hitter when, as he said, "I stopped acting as though every trip to the plate was a life-or-death proposition."

Even so, Schmidt had never liked hitting in Wrigley. Although the park was small, and when the wind was right, pop-ups could go over the outfield fence, Schmidt could never seem to catch a break there. He had only five homers at Wrigley in three years.

Once the game began, if there was anyone more anxious to get out of town than Schmidt, it must have been Phillies' pitcher Steve Carlton. Carlton was taking a pounding on this windy April day, as the Cubs had jumped out to a 12-1 lead by the third inning. Then things started to get a little crazy.

In the fifth inning, Schmidt homered with a man on. Then in the seventh, he hit a solo home run. By now it was 13-7, and Schmidt was starting to feel pretty good.

The Phillies had cut it to 13-9 by the eighth inning, when Schmidt came to the plate again. This time there were two men on. Schmidt crushed the pitch into the center field bleachers to make it 13-12. The Phillies improbable rally continued in the ninth, as they took the lead, 15-13. Then it was the Cubs turn to rally. They scored two runs to send the game into extra innings.

Schmidt returned to the plate in the tenth inning with one runner on. Again he smashed a ball into the center field bleachers, his fourth home run of the game. The Phillies would hold on for an 18-16 win, tying the National League record for the biggest comeback in a game. Schmidt had become just the sixth player in National League history to homer four times in a game, and the first since Willie Mays had done it in 1961.

Among all the celebration in the clubhouse, though, Schmidt kept his head. "When a batter strikes out four times in a game, they tell him to forget it," he said afterward. "Well, I'd like to forget about the homers. I want to concentrate on the games ahead."

Schmidt did just that, leading the league in homers for the third straight season, on his way to a career total of 548. **TS**

# A Spectacular Charge at a Magic Mark

I t had been such a magical season, a year in which fly balls dropped just beyond the reach of outfielders, ground balls scooted safely through infields, and every pitch looked big, fat, and straight down the middle for George Brett.

Hitting over .400 seemed almost easy in the summer of 1980; it seemed odd that no one had hit the magic mark since Ted Williams in 1941. Through June, July, and August, every thing seemed to come together for Brett. Sure, he was nagged by a few minor injuries, which would force him to miss several games. But that didn't seem to matter much. His team, the Kansas City Royals, was running away with the Western Division title, and everything Brett hit seemed to fall in for a base hit.

By late August, Brett was hitting .407 and having a blast. He loved winning, and he loved being the center of attention. It seemed as if everyone wanted to talk to him. He held a press conference *before* each game, and he had a crowd of reporters around his locker *after* each game. Brett was always accommodating and entertaining. He would tell reporters he was having the time of his life.

Then things began to change. As September dragged on, his batting average began to sink. It was getting tougher and tougher to scratch out a hit. Drives that once cleared the outfield fences were dying into the waiting gloves of outfielders; line drives weren't finding their way out of the infield.

Yes, the crowd of writers still followed him around. Only now they were asking about things Brett didn't want to talk about. Could he still do it? Why was he slumping?

On a West Coast road trip, Brett went into a lengthy slump. He was pressing now and it showed. In 20 at bats he had just 3 hits. Great fun? For Brett, the chase had now become a nightmare.

Breaking the .400 mark had been an obsession, one that was hard to forget when you had a dozen or so reporters asking about it every day. Royals' manager Jim Frey could see the changes in Brett, and knew he had to do something. On a Sunday game against the Minnesota Twins, Frey gave Brett the day off. It was the best move he could have made.

Brett had been agonizing over the chase. Now he had a chance to put it in perspective. He decided to put the .400 mark out of his mind and concentrate on just having fun. Sitting on the bench, he laughed, he joked, he pulled pranks, all the things he didn't do during his slump. The Royals were glad to see him smiling again, even if he never got another hit.

Then came the sixth inning. Frey put Brett in as a pinch-hitter with the bases loaded. Frey and the Royals were amazed by Brett's casualness as he walked to the plate. They were also amazed as Brett stroked a grand slam, making it look almost easy. They knew he was back.

Brett fell short of the magic .400, number, but he made a spectacular charge at it. He batted .390—the highest anyone had hit since Ted Williams hit .406 39 years before. Brett was somewhat disappointed, of course, having come so close to the magic mark. Yet, he wasn't disappointed for too long.

In the playoffs, Brett launched a home run into the third deck at Yankee Stadium to cap a Royals' sweep of the Yankees in the American League Championship Series. The Royals had finally made it to the World Series, and George Brett knew he was a major reason why they got there.　**TS**

# Index